# MIDWAY 1942

◄ *Wildcat and Dauntless aircraft of the U.S. carrier* Enterprise *are armed and fueled prior to launch, sometime during May or June 1942. (U.S. Navy)*

**Kaga.** *Together with Akagi, Kaga formed the First Division of the carriers of the First Air Fleet. Its huge size was remarked upon by several of the U.S. Navy pilots who bombed her. Illustration by Jan Suermondt.*

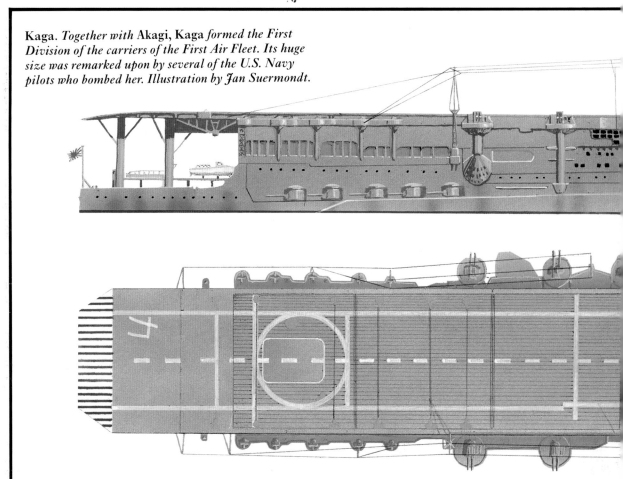

CONSULTANT EDITOR: DAVID G. CHANDLER

GROLIER OSPREY | MODERN CAMPAIGNS | 8

# MIDWAY 1942

## TURNING POINT IN THE PACIFIC

**MARK HEALY**

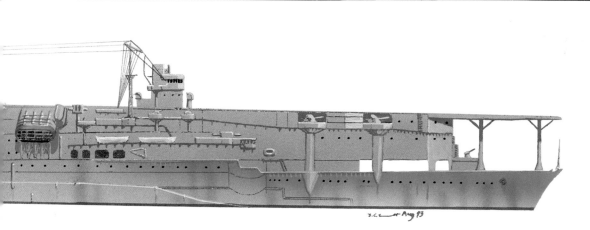

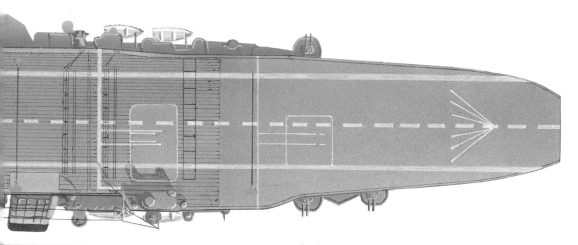

Published 1997 by Grolier
Educational, Danbury, Connecticut
06816.
Published for the school and library
market exclusively by Grolier
Educational.

Set ISBN 0-7172-7678-3
Volume ISBN 0-7172-7675-9

Cataloging information to be obtained
directly from Grolier Educational

Produced by DAG Publications Ltd
Color birds's eye view illustrations by
Peter Harper. Cartography by
Micromap.
*Wargaming Midway by* Bob Cordery.
Wargames consultant Duncan
Macfarlane.
Typeset by Dorchester Typesetting
Group Ltd, Dorchester, Dorset. Mono
camerawork by M&E Reproductions,
North Fambridge, Essex. Printed
in Hong Kong.

# CONTENTS

◄ *American SBDs and TBDs prepare to launch from* **Enterprise,** *the launch officer making signals to the pilot of the first Dauntless. This photograph was taken in May 1942, and the aircraft are devoid of offensive armament apart from two small practice bombs carried by the SBD. (via Robert Dorr)*

*Two images symbolizing the triumph of Japanese arms in the opening six months of the Pacific War. In the first, victorious Imperial Army soldiers raise their arms in a* banzai *salute following the fall of Corregidor in May 1942. Such victories did much to foster a sense of invincibility in the Japanese Army and Combined Fleet that was to contribute in no small measure to the defeat at Midway (via Robert F. Dorr). The second shows the stricken battleship USS* Arizona, *sunk and ablaze following the surprise Japanese air attack on Pearl Harbor on 7 December 1941.*

# PRELUDE TO MIDWAY

In the history of war there have been few military operations in which the trifling material damage inflicted on an enemy has been so totally outweighed by its attendant psychological impact, and the ensuing strategic consequences, as in the Doolittle raid on Japan on 18 April 1942. The audacity of the raid served to demonstrate that, in spite of the remarkable victories that had been achieved by the Imperial Army and Navy in Southeast Asia since the outbreak of war, the United States remained capable of striking at the heart of the Japanese empire, ridiculing the pretension that territorial conquest had in any way rendered the homeland inviolable.

The Japanese nation's outrage at the raid was compounded by the loss of face experienced by the Imperial Navy. It saw its ability to exercise responsibility for the defense of the seas around Japan, and thereby ensure the safety of the Emperor, impugned. These sentiments were echoed by Admiral Isoroku Yamamoto, Commander in Chief of the Combined Fleet, whose own concern to prevent Tokyo being attacked from the air verged on the obsessional. "One has the embarrassing feeling of having been caught napping just when one was feeling confident and in charge of things," he said. "Even though there wasn't much damage, it is a disgrace that the skies of the Imperial capital should have been defiled without a single enemy plane being shot down." More significantly, while the Japanese authorities outwardly ridiculed the attack as the "do-nothing" or "do-little" raid, the collective disquiet of the Naval General Staff and the planners of the Combined Fleet was sufficient to end their irresolution concerning the detailed timetable appending the decision to launch Operation MI.

On 5 May Admiral Osami Nagano, the Chief of the Naval General Staff, issued Imperial GHQ Naval Order No. 18 instructing Yamamoto to "carry

▶ *Lieutenant Colonel James H. Doolittle poses for the camera with Marc Mitscher, captain of USS* Hornet, *shortly before the famous raid on Japan that bore his name. The raid was to have consequences far beyond the limited damage it inflicted on the targets struck in Japan. (U.S. National Archives)*

out the occupation of Midway Islands and key points in the western Aleutians." One month later the Combined Fleet, convinced of certain victory, had put to sea the largest and most powerful naval force since Jutland. Nevertheless, it was to experience in the Battle of Midway a defeat so decisive as to doom itself and the cause of Imperial Japan to inevitable ruin. That such an outcome was even possible at a time when Japan's military success was at its zenith requires understanding of the strategic context governing decisions pertaining to future operations by the Combined Fleet in the months following Pearl Harbor. This, in turn, draws us to an appreciation of the central role in such planning played by Fleet Admiral Yamamoto, whose strategic perspective was fundamental in the provision of the rationale for, the planning of and execution of Operation MI.

### Then What Will Come Next?

On the first day of 1942 Rear Admiral Matome Ugaki penned the following thoughts in his personal diary: "It has been only twenty-five days since the war started, yet operations have been progressing smoothly and we have enough reason to hope for the completion of the first stage of the war before the end of March. Then what will come next?" That the Chief of Staff of the Combined

*Opposite page, top: The first of the 16 USAAF B-25 Mitchells start their engines as the crews board their aircraft shortly before launching, 18 April 1942. (U.S. National Archives)*

*Opposite page, center: Having been discovered by a Japanese picket vessel stationed to guard the western sea approaches to Japan, Admiral Halsey was forced to launch the Doolittle force at a range of 824 miles, rather than the intended 650 miles. The unforeseen benefit of this decision was that the*

*Doolittle force arrived over targets virtually unopposed by Japanese air or ground forces. (U.S. National Archives)*

*Opposite page, bottom: "Scratch one flat top!" In the battle of the Coral Sea in May 1942 the U.S. Navy was able to sink the Japanese light carrier Shoho. In this photograph taken by a Yorktown aircraft it is possible to see a TBD that has just launched its torpedo on the extreme right of the picture. (U.S. National Archives)*

Fleet could utter such a question less than a month after his nation had plunged headlong into war with the United States and Great Britain speaks volumes for the lack of any long-term strategic vision appending that decision. The absence of such was not surprising, given that the motivations governing Imperial Japan's choice of war in December 1941 to resolve its economic problems hardly rested on any rational appraisal of the actual or potential forces she had chosen to oppose. Indeed, the need to secure oil supplies had become so central in driving the formulation of Japan's initial war strategy, and the risks attendant upon its realization so great, that little thought had been given by her strategists to what would follow, when and if success was achieved.

With a remarkable economy of force comprising 11 divisions, some 1,200 aircraft and most of the navy, in the 100 days following Pearl Harbor Japan proceeded to humble the military forces of the United States, Australia, the Netherlands and Great Britain. By the end of March, as Ugaki had predicted, the Japanese had essentially achieved their initial war aims of securing control over the oil supplies of the Dutch East Indies, and widening the defensive perimeter around the homeland. Furthermore, the material cost of achieving this had been extraordinarily low. Having allowed for fleet losses of at least 25 percent, the Navy lost only 23 vessels amounting to barely 10 percent of the anticipated figure. In the four months in which Japan's armed forces had run rampant across the western Pacific and Southeast Asia, she had shown that her soldiers, sailors, warships and aircraft were equal, if not superior, to those of her despised and supposedly superior enemies. Consequently, few in Japan or in the armed forces would have disputed the view expressed by Ugaki in his diary entry at the onset of the new year: ". . . the future is filled with brightness . . . The course of events during this year will determine the fate of the war, so we must work hard, exerting every effort. The main thing is to win, and we surely will win." Translating these sentiments into reality was the task delegated to Ugaki by Admiral Yamamoto, when told to begin the planning of second-stage strategy immediately.

It was symptomatic of the relative ineffectualness of the Imperial General Headquarters (IGHQ),

# Operations AL and MI

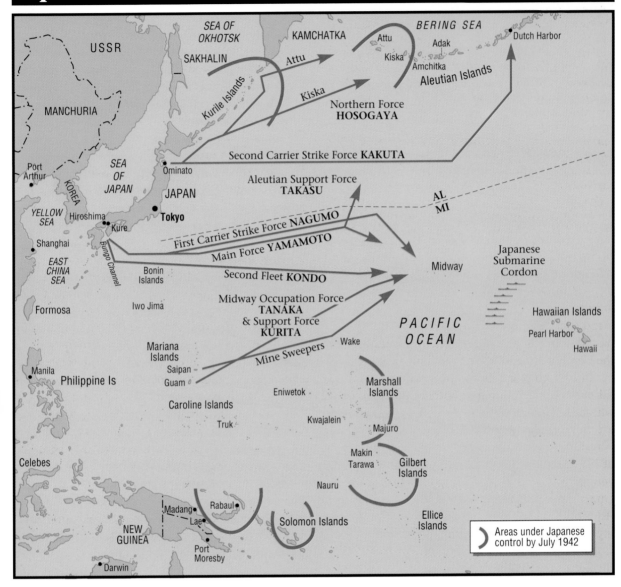

the body responsible for the formulation of the nation's war strategy, that Admiral Yamamoto, as head of the Combined Fleet, could abrogate this major task to himself. However, although the IGHQ comprised the General Staffs of the Army and the Navy under the supreme command of the Emperor, it was rent by a rivalry that never allowed the emergence of a coherent strategy governing the operations of both services. In reality IGHQ presided over two essentially distinct strategy-making bodies. The army, as the senior of the two services, always perceived that its primary focus and Japan's true

interests lay in China and the defense of Manchuria against a greatly feared Soviet threat. This focus meant that its support for the "southern" strategy, which drove the conflict started on 7 December 1941, was heavily conditional on the degree to which it served the army's interests in its primary theater of operations in China, and on the limited number of army divisions it was grudgingly prepared to employ in support of essentially "naval" operations in this new theater of war. Compounding the army's relative indifference to strategic questions beyond its own sphere of interest was the decline in the

◄ *This map illustrates the maximum expansion of Imperial Japan after Operations MI and AL and the decisive defeat suffered by the Combined Fleet (Rengo Kantai) in the Battle of Midway. As such it shows the only territorial acquisitions made as a consequence of that disastrous enterprise, the two remote Aleutian Islands of Attu and Kiska. Had Midway fallen then it, too, would have been added to the forward Eastern Pacific defense line running from the Aleutians through* *Midway, Wake Island, the Marshalls and the Gilbert Islands down to Port Moresby in New Guinea. Had the Japanese won the battle, then it is known that Yamamoto would have pressed the Imperial Government to proffer peace proposals to the United States. These would almost certainly have been based on their acquiescence to the territorial conquests made by Japan since December 1941 and in the permanency of the outer defense perimeter.*

influence of the Naval General Staff and its command over the formulations of naval strategy, which passed in practice from itself to the planning staff of the Combined Fleet under Admiral Yamamoto.

In part, this arose from the dynamic and powerful personality of the Combined Fleet Commander, who held a low opinion of the abilities of his superior, the Chief of the Naval General Staff. Admiral Nagano rarely involved himself in the formulation of Naval Staff strategy. He tended to leave it to the younger officers of the Plans Division of the First Operations Section under the command of Rear Admiral Fukudome. Consequently his role increasingly became that of umpire when the views of Combined Fleet and his own Plans Division conflicted, as in the dispute before the Pearl Harbor Operation, which was strongly opposed by members of his own staff. Nagano had given final approval to Yamamoto's Pearl Harbor plan, even though it was in his domain to reject it, in spite of the latter's threat to resign unless the General Staff accepted it.

While this could be interpreted as acquiescence to blackmail, it was also deference on Nagano's part to one whose abilities he recognized as being indispensable to the Navy. In a most revealing observation it was said: "Nagano had the utmost confidence in Yamamoto's abilities and judgment. He finally agreed because he knew Yamamoto was not bluffing. If this seems strange it must be remembered that

Yamamoto's position and influence in the Japanese Navy were unique. He was in truth a leviathan among men." Given the success of the Pearl Harbor attack, it is therefore not surprising that his prestige was now such that the formulation of strategy by the Combined Fleet's staff officers under Yamamoto's guidance was tacitly presumed and accepted.

This is not to suggest, however, that the Naval General Staff were simply prepared to acquiesce to Yamamoto designs. There remained in the Plans Division fertile minds who not only advocated their own strategy, but were prepared to fight their corner and, if necessary, oppose the demands of Yamamoto and his planning staff. Even so, as events were to show, it was a forlorn hope to believe that they could deflect the Combined Fleet commander from his chosen course once his mind was made up.

When Ugaki emerged from his cabin on 14 January to present the outcome of his deliberations, he prefaced his recommendations with the crucial observation that Japan could not afford to rest on its laurels by consolidating on its initial conquests. To do so would hand over the initiative for the offensive, allowing the United States to increase its strength while Japan waited passively for the Americans to attack. Under such circumstances the proven effectiveness and technical proficiency of the Imperial Navy would rapidly become a wasting asset. To capitalize on the strategic advantage created by the Combined Fleet in its initial war operations, Japan needed to resume the offensive. Governed by this rationale, Ugaki evaluated a number of operational possibilities. He finally proposed that Japan should seize the islands of Midway, Johnston and Palmyra with a view to transforming them into advanced air bases before an invasion of Hawaii. He argued that such an operation was likely to precipitate that decisive battle with the U.S. fleet that still lay at the core of Japanese naval strategy. His proposal was rejected by Captain Kuroshima, the Senior Fleet Operations Officer, because he doubted whether the U.S. would risk its fleet to save these islands. He then proffered his own recommendation, shifting the strategic focus of the Combined Fleet westward toward the Indian Ocean and an operation to seize Ceylon (Sri Lanka). While accepting the critique of his own proposals and approving Kuroshima's, Ugaki insisted on the proviso that an Indian Ocean operation be carried out within the context of a joint Axis under-taking, with the Japanese second-stage offensive "timed to synchronize with German Offensives in the Near and Middle East." What might have constituted a major strategic opportunity came to nought, however, when the Germans made no offer of joint operations in the new Tripartite Axis military agreement signed on 19 December. Never-theless, Combined Fleet continued to explore Kuroshima's proposal as a purely Japanese under-taking. Following war games on the new flagship *Yamato* in February, the western operation was adopted by the Naval General Staff as the official Naval proposal for phase two strategy. It was pre-sented as such to a joint conference at IGHQ in mid March, only to be scuppered by the army when it became obvious that the operation depended upon the supply of more divisions for the amphibious assault on Ceylon.

Remaining committed to the need for offensive action, Combined Fleet cast around for an alterna-tive plan. It returned to Ugaki's initial proposal for action in the eastern Pacific, reworked to exclude the possibility of an army veto. The plan now evolved dropped the ambitious suggestion to invade Hawaii, and required an invasion of the western Aleutians and Midway Island. Not least among the factors shaping Combined Fleet's decision by this time were the decidedly unwelcome, though tactically insignificant, U.S. attacks on the Marshalls, Rabaul, Wake, eastern New Guinea and Marcus Island from February onward. With the last-named island only 1,000 miles from Tokyo and within the outer ring of Japan's defenses, the continued survival of the U.S. carriers allowed the Americans the option of using them for a strike on the homeland. This prospect obsessed the deeply patriotic Yamamoto, and the continued operation of the U.S. carriers threw into sharp focus the need to finish the work begun at Pearl Harbor by ensuring their belated destruction.

This was the rationale for the Midway opera-tion, and it is known that, if it could be achieved, Yamamoto intended to use his undoubted prestige to press Japan's political leaders to make peace over-tures to the Allies. Yamamoto believed that victory at Midway would provide him with a strategic edge that would allow Japan to negotiate from a position of strength, and thus force the enemy to come to terms. He was ever conscious of the latent power of the United States and Japan's relative weakness, and his absolute commitment to the Midway offensive was governed by the overwhelming conviction that, unless victory could be realized quickly and when Japanese power was at its zenith, the alternative for his beloved country was defeat in a long war. There can be little wonder that, when faced with such awe-some possibilities, he would brook no criticism or diversion from his chosen path.

The Naval General Staff had also been review-ing options following the army's veto on the Ceylon operation. From within the Plans Division there emerged the view that Combined Fleet and the army should concentrate on a major operation directed at Australia – the *Bei Go Shaden Sakusen*. This proposal was predicated on the assumption that Australia was the logical base for an Allied counteroffensive in the south seas. As such it would become the recipient of vast quantities of Allied and particularly American armaments as their forces built up their strength. To negate this potential threat to Japan's southern flank required either that parts of Australia should be occupied, or, at least, that steps be taken to isolate the subcontinent from the U.S. As the former possibility depended on the army stumping up the necessary divisions for the operation, it is not surprising that it, too, went the way of the Ceylon proposal. Even so, the Naval General Staff believed there was sufficient merit in the second proposal for it to proceed to formulate a more limited operation designed to isolate Australia by extending Japanese control over eastern New Guinea and the Solomon Islands. The Naval Gen-eral Staff proceeded to organize the necessary forces to launch an amphibious operation, codenamed MO, to occupy the island of Tulagi in the Solomons and, more importantly, to seize Port Moresby on the southeastern coast of New Guinea. To the naval forces earmarked for this operation Yamamoto added Carrier Division 5, comprising the new fleet carriers *Shokaku* and *Zuikaku*, believing that the Americans would deploy a carrier Task Force to oppose the Japanese. As events were to show, Yamamoto was proffering a hostage to fortune, as the initial planning for the Midway operation pre-sumed that these two vessels would be available to serve with the Nagumo force.

By the end of March the Combined Fleet plan for the Midway campaign was complete and had been presented to the Naval General Staff on 2 April by Yamamoto's loyal and trusted aides, Captains Watanabe and Kuroshima. Over the next three days there was much heated and fervent discussion as these two officers debated the merit of the Midway operation with those in the Plans Division of the General Staff who opposed it. Matters came to a head on 5 April, when Watanabe restated Yamamoto's unambiguous support for the Midway operation by echoing his master's voice: "In the last analysis, the success or failure of our entire strategy in the Pacific will be determined by whether or not we succeed in destroying the United States Fleet, particularly its aircraft carriers . . . We believe that by launching the proposed operations against Midway we can succeed in drawing out the enemy's carrier fleet and destroying it in decisive battle. If, on the other hand, the enemy should avoid our challenge, we shall still realize an important gain by advancing our defensive perimeter to Midway and the western Aleutians without obstruction."

To emphasize his unwillingness to compromise, Yamamoto once again played his resignation gambit. In the face of Yamamoto's resolute stand, Rear Admiral Fukudome expressed the view: "If the C in C is so set on it, shall we leave it to him?" Nagano raised no objection, instructing a shift of resources to the Midway operation. Once the plan was adopted by the Naval General Staff the army, given how few troops it would be required to allocate, was more than happy to endorse Operations MI and AL, as the Midway and Aleutian offensives now became known, and thus also passed IGHQ scrutiny on the nod. There now only remained the debate concerning the details of the operation, with Combined Fleet wishing for the earliest practicable date and the Naval General Staff wishing for a delay. So matters continued until 18 April, when Jimmy Doolittle's B-25s roared over Tokyo, bringing further discussion to a rapid conclusion.

## Victory Disease

It is apparent that, by this time, Japanese thinking had become afflicted by a canker "so great that its effects may be found on every level of the planning and execution of the Midway Operation," and which was to have a profound impact on the out-

▼ *Sailors aboard one of the heavy cruisers of the screening force of TF-17 observe the evacuation of the crew of the listing and burning carrier USS* Lexington *in the Coral Sea on 7 May 1942. Hit by bombs and torpedoes, the* Lexington *was later to founder following a series of massive internal explosions. Nevertheless, the U.S. Navy had realized a strategic victory by halting the Combined Fleet's attempt to capture Port Moresby in New Guinea. It was the first time that a Japanese offensive had been stopped. (via Robert F. Dorr)*

come of the battle. The emergence of what later became diagnosed as "victory disease" had its origins in the unique quasi-mythological view the Japanese had of themselves and their nation, which they believed was destined to become *Sekai Dai Ichi*, or "First in the World." The Japanese saw in the invulnerability of their sacred homeland evidence of their undisputed military effectiveness. Significantly, this and her successes in conflicts before the outbreak of the Pacific War were explained away in Japan less by reference to material and technical factors than by stressing the moral dimension in war. This engendered a mindset wherein it was believed that the *Nihon Seishin* – the innate Japanese spirit – would allow the nation to triumph over any enemy.

For a Japan imbued with the martial virtues of the Samurai tradition, the denigration of the United States as weak, decadent and effete convinced many that there was little to fear in taking on this great western power. This flawed perception of the United States fostered a profound underestimation of the immense military, industrial and, indeed, moral potential of that nation which in the longer term was to prove fatal for Japan. In the immediate circumstance, however, the remarkable victories of the opening four months of the Pacific War served only to compound the arrogant attitude of the Japanese toward their enemies, and "by the time of the Midway battle this arrogance had reached a point where it permeated the thinking and actions of officers and men in the fighting services."

Directly arising from this, and affecting the highest echelons of the Navy, including Yamamoto himself, was the *idée fixe* that the Japanese possessed the undoubted initiative in the forthcoming operation. In consequence it was presumed, to the point that it became an article of faith, that the U.S. Fleet would put to sea only subsequent to the invasion and occupation of Midway. The notion that their carriers might be at sea awaiting the Japanese Fleet, although recognized as a possibility, defied credulity. Indeed, when such a possibility was broached during the Midway war games held on the *Yamato* between 1–4 May to explore the coming battle, the consequences of such an eventuality were dismissed in a remarkably cavalier fashion.

Fuchida and Okumiya related how, when asked to explain how the First Carrier Striking Force

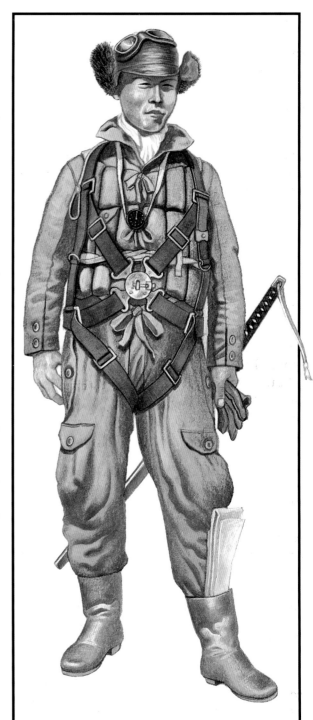

*This pilot of the Imperial Japanese Navy is in summer flying gear, wearing a fur-lined leather flying helmet, one-piece green cotton flying suit and leather flying boots. White silk scarves were common among pilots. Officers of the rank of lieutenant commander or higher carried their swords in action. Illustration by Chris Warner.*

would deal with such an eventuality, Minoru Genda, the normally highly astute and level headed aviation specialist, replied in such a vague fashion as to imply that there existed no plan to deal with such a contingency. Although Rear Admiral Ugaki remonstrated over the matter, he nevertheless revealed his own inner certainty of victory when, later in the games, he arbitrarily overturned the decision of the umpire who had ruled that the carriers *Kaga* and *Akagi* were sunk, so that only the former was dispatched while the latter emerged from battle with only light damage. Furthermore, as the games led on to explore the post-Midway operations, *Kaga* was miraculously resurrected from its watery grave! Other examples of this overweening optimism included the seaplane squadron that sent a remarkably careless signal to the effect that it wished all mail to be forwarded to Midway from mid-June. Possibly the most extreme example of this attitude was evidenced in a statement by a spokesman for the Naval General Staff, who contemptuously stated: "What we are most concerned about is that the enemy will be loath to meet our fleet and will refuse to come out from his base."

## Final Preparations

Against this backdrop, preparations for the Midway and subsidiary Aleutians operations gained strength as April turned to May. The First Air Fleet had returned to Japan from their Indian Ocean venture on 22 April to hear of the first news of MI and begin refurbishment and training for the operation. They were but four warships in an immense fleet of nearly 200 vessels assembled by Yamamoto for the Midway operation. By the midmonth, however, as the cost of the Battle of the Coral Sea became apparent, Nagumo knew that he would be taking two fewer fleet carriers with him to Midway than originally intended. For, notwithstanding the great victory trumpeted by the Japanese media, the carrier *Shokaku* had been so severely damaged that her repairs would take many months to complete, and her sister ship *Zuikaku* had lost so many of her aircrew that she could not take part in MI because of a lack of replacements.

Although the Japanese regarded the setback of their naval assault on Port Moresby as a short-term

frustration, their compensation lay in the conviction that they had imposed heavy losses on the Allied Task Forces. Certain enemy losses proclaimed by the home media included a Saratoga-class carrier (in reality the *Lexington*) and the USS *Yorktown*. The latter, left sinking and later presumed sunk, was removed from Japan's estimate of the U.S. Navy's order of battle, but was to reappear barely a month later to make a significant contribution to the outcome of the Battle of Midway.

Matters now began to move more quickly as the different elements in the great plan started to move in accordance with the complex timetable. On 21 May Yamamoto led the battleships of his Main Body, Nagumo's four fleet carriers and Kondo's Second Fleet, to sea to begin two days of what would prove to be the final fleet maneuvers ever staged by the Combined Fleet. Final war games held on the *Yamato* on 24 May, rehearsing both the Midway and the Aleutians offensives, showed that operations would proceed smoothly. On the same day the Midway invasion group of transports carrying the army assault troops of Colonel Kiyonao Ichicki rendezvoused at Saipan with the heavy cruisers of Rear Admiral Kurita's Support Force. The forces earmarked for the AL operation made their way to the Ominato naval base in Northern Honshu before sortieing on 28 May.

All was now ready for the departure of the largest assemblage of vessels ever seen in the Pacific. For those aboard the many ships of the armada there was little doubt of the momentous nature of the occasion. Shortly after 0800 on the morning of 28 May the *Akagi* struck the signal flag ordering the First Air Fleet to up anchor and sortie as planned. To the accompaniment of the cheers and the myriad waving caps of the crews of the battleships of Yamamoto's Main Body, the 21 warships wound their way in line ahead through the Bungo Channel and out into the open sea. No better insight into the sense of invincibility now pervading the Nagumo Force can be offered than the final intelligence assessment which the commanding admiral presented to his crews as they were preparing to close on Midway Island some days later:

"The enemy is unaware of our presence in this area and will remain so until after our initial attacks on the island."

# THE U.S. PREPARATIONS

Yamamoto and Nagumo were sure that they would achieve tactical if not strategic surprise, but they would not have been so sanguine had they known that the Americans had wind of the Midway operation as early as the beginning of April. Although there were suspicions, it was only after the war that the Japanese would discover for certain that Operation MI had been fatally compromised as a consequence of a remarkable American intelligence coup that gave them detailed knowledge of the Japanese plan.

While many other factors were to come into play before victory was delivered to the Americans at Midway, none ranks so high as the breaking of JN25, the Japanese Navy's current operational code. Although this was a remarkable achievement, the code was not understood in its entirety. Nevertheless, sufficient phrases could be read to allow Commander Joseph Rochefort, commander of the Navy Combat Intelligence Office outstation on Hawaii (known as "Hypo"), to inform Fleet Admiral Chester Nimitz that the Japanese were preparing a very large operation which he was convinced was directed at Midway. Although the intelligence was initially ambiguous enough to allow for other interpretations of Japanese intentions, Nimitz was sufficiently convinced of the case presented by Rochefort to start planning on the basis that Midway was the Japanese target. He had already learned to value Rochefort's judgment, having won his spurs in April, when, on the basis of existing intelligence, he had forecast the Japanese operation to take Port Moresby. By acting on this and other intelligence sources, Nimitz had dispatched Task Forces 11 and 17 which, for the loss of the *Lexington*, stopped the southward advance of the Combined Fleet.

On 2 May Nimitz made an inspection tour of Midway Island. Although at this juncture he did not enlighten either Lieutenant Commander Shannon

Commander Cyril Simmard, the two senior officers in command there, as to his suspicions, he did ascertain from them what would be needed to hold off a major amphibious assault. On his return to Pearl Harbor he penned them a letter to the effect that the Japanese intended to launch a major attack on Midway Island on or about 28 May. Subsequently manpower and air power on the atoll base was increased to a level that Shannon believed sufficient

▲ *Commander Joseph Rochefort was to provide the Americans with an invaluable intelligence coup when he and his SIGINT team on Hawaii cracked the essentials of the Japanese Navy code* *JN25. It was this breakthrough that was to lead the American Naval historian Samuel Morison subsequently to label Midway as "a victory of intelligence." (U.S. Navy)*

to hold out against any amphibious assault. Within a few days, however, Nimitz was presented with vital intelligence which established beyond doubt that Midway, and not Hawaii or the ̲eastern coast of the United States, was the objective of the coming Japanese offensive. He was thus able to declare, on 14 May, a state of "fleet opposed invasion" for the Hawaii area including Midway. Once again it was "Hypo" and the resourceful Commander Rochefort who provided him with confirming evidence of enemy intentions.

The clinch came as the result of a ruse by Rochefort. In their interbase communications the Japanese used code letters to designate what were clearly locations, but which code for which location? From other information appended to the code it was inferred that the use of "AL," for instance, was a reference to the Aleutians, but "AF" was less certain, although Rochefort was sure it was Midway. To flush out the Japanese, Rochefort secured permission from Nimitz for a message to be sent in plain English from Midway, reporting that there was a water shortage on the island.

As the island lacked any natural water supply, its occupants were dependent upon a water filtration plant that was reported as having blown up. The request for fresh water to be delivered by tanker would thus ring true to Japanese eavesdroppers, for whose benefit the false message was despatched. Two days later, on 12 May, the Hypo team were rewarded by the Japanese broadcasting to their own fleet commanders that "AF is short of water." Notwithstanding the niggles that continued to come from Admiral King in Washington concerning the likely target of the Japanese attack, Nimitz was now convinced beyond any doubt that Midway was truly the objective of Yamamoto's massive enterprise. He proceeded to harness his own limited air and naval assets to frustrate Japanese intentions.

On 15 May Vice Admiral William Halsey, commander of Task Force 16 comprising the carriers *Enterprise* and *Hornet*, was recalled by Nimitz to Pearl Harbor from the vicinity of the Solomon Islands, where he had arrived too late to take part in the Coral Sea battle. Nimitz had intended to give command of the Midway Task Force to Halsey, but on the latter's return to Pearl on the 26th it was clear that his very poor physical condition preclud-

ed this. A chronic skin complaint diagnosed as "general dermatitis" denied a deeply disappointed Halsey the opportunity to take his "major crack at the Japs." However, he served Nimitz and his country proud when he unhesitatingly recommended that his replacement be Rear Admiral Raymond A. Spruance. Although he was not an airman, both Halsey and Nimitz held the man in very high regard, and neither had any compunction about placing Task Force 16 in his hands.

In his initial briefing with him, Nimitz told Spruance that he would need to sortie on the 28th, as some days earlier Rochefort and his Hypo team had informed him of the coming Midway offensive and stated that the Japanese had postponed D-Day until 3 June at the earliest. This was only part of a much larger message that Hypo had deciphered just before the Japanese changed the JN25 code, which revealed itself to be nothing more than the principal details of their order of battle for the coming operation. In consequence Nimitz was able to tell Spruance more or less exactly what he was up against, and the general direction from which the Japanese carriers would be approaching Midway. Nimitz was thus in a position to present to Spruance his operational plan for the Task Forces 16 and 17, predicated on the intelligence provided by Hypo.

The following day Nimitz also met with Rear Admiral Frank Fletcher, who had just brought the heavily damaged *Yorktown* limping back into Pearl. Without revealing his sources, Nimitz informed him of the Japanese intention to seize Midway Island and said that they would be employing at least four carriers and many supporting vessels in the operation organized into Nagumo's carrier strike force, a support force and the invasion force. Nimitz then told Fletcher that he would be putting to sea again in the *Yorktown* within a few days to join up with Spruance to the northeast of Midway Island, whereupon he would assume tactical command of Task Forces 16 and 17.

However, this presupposed that the *Yorktown* would be sufficiently repaired to be able to sortie on time. Many who surveyed her damage doubted that it could be done. Estimates of time needed for repairs ranged from a pessimistic three months to Fletcher's own more optimistic prediction of two weeks. If the latter figure was correct, *Yorktown* would not be available for the coming battle and Spruance would face Nagumo with two, rather than three, carriers – not a wide enough margin to encourage hopes of success.

In a remarkable demonstration of American improvisation the carrier was taken into dry dock, where some 1,400 dockyard workers descended upon the vessel en masse and set to preparing her for sea, working around the clock. To the sound of

*This Marine Corps pilot wears the A-4 summer flying suit and A-8 summer helmet. He is also sporting a Navy-issue shoulder holster, worn here slung at the hip. Illustration by Chris Warner.*

▶ *Such was the damage inflicted on the USS* Yorktown *in the Battle of the Coral Sea that the Imperial Navy presumed her sunk. Limping back to Pearl Harbor on 27 May she was placed in Dry Dock No. 1 and returned to service within a remarkable 48 hours. Although her many repairs were temporary at best, her presence at Midway was to prove decisive. (via Roger Chesneau)*

pneumatic hammers and by the light of welders' torches the *Yorktown*'s hull was patched up and her damaged compartments strengthened with timbers. Few of the watertight doors worked owing to frames being buckled by Japanese bomb damage, but on Saturday 29 May – the day after Spruance had sailed with Task Force 16 – Fletcher put to sea in the *Yorktown*. Her hastily assembled air group comprised squadrons from no fewer than three

carriers. Along with her escorts, the heavy cruisers *Astoria* and *Portland* and the six destroyers of DesRon 2, the *Yorktown* moved north from Oahu at a stately 27kts, the highest speed her damaged engines could produce, to rendezvous with *Enterprise* and *Hornet*. Barring any unforeseen eventuality, Fletcher felt confident he could satisfy Nimitz's heartfelt exhortation that Task Forces 16 and 17 rendezvous to the northeast of Midway on time.

# THE OPPOSING PLANS

## The Japanese Plan

The aims governing Operations AL and MI were twofold. First, to establish a new forward defense line running from the Aleutians through Midway, Wake Island, the Marshalls, the Gilbert Islands and the southern Solomons to Port Moresby, and, secondly and more importantly, to effect the destruction of the remaining surface units of the U.S. Fleet in that "decisive fleet engagement in the Pacific," or *Kassen Kantai*, so dear to the hearts of Japanese Naval strategists. This was to be precipitated by the invasion and occupation of the island of Midway, a base the Japanese believed to be of such strategic importance to the U.S. Navy that it would be forced to sortie from Hawaii with the remaining warships of the Pacific Fleet to challenge Japan's occupation of it. Certain of realizing at least tactical surprise and disposing of an overwhelming superiority in warships, Combined Fleet was confident of a decisive victory in the naval battle that would follow.

To achieve this end, Combined Fleet had formulated a complex and critically timed plan involving a two-pronged offensive. The execution of the different phases of both offensives turned on 7 June, designated as N-Day (the Japanese equivalent of the U.S. D-Day). This had been chosen by Combined Fleet as the earliest practicable date that would allow the Nagumo Fleet to recuperate following its return to Japan from its Indian Ocean operation, as well as being the last day in June when there would be sufficient moonlight to allow an amphibious landing on Midway Island at night.

The first and lesser of the two offensives, codenamed AL, was a diversionary operation against the Aleutian islands in the Northern Pacific. The brief given to Vice Admiral Hosogaya for AL required the neutralization of U.S. air power at Dutch Harbor beginning on 3 June, three days before N-Day, followed by the occupation over a succession of days of the islands of Adak, Kiska and Attu through to 12 June. Forces allocated to AL included Northern Force Main Body, the Second Carrier Striking Force, the Attu and Kiska Invasion Forces and a submarine unit detached to assist the Aleutians operation. In addition, Combined Fleet had allocated, as a detachment from Yamamoto's Main Body, a screening force of battleships for the Aleutian operation under the command of Vice Admiral Takasu. Whereas the latter would sortie from the main Fleet anchorage in Hashirajima Bay along with the rest of the Main Body under Yamamoto on 29 May, the others would depart from the Ominato Naval Base in northern Honshu a day earlier.

The MI operation fell into two distinct phases, with the participating fleet elements all playing their role according to a very tightly orchestrated timetable. Phase 1 involved the occupation of Midway Island itself on N-Day. Thereafter, it was presumed that the disposition of the Fleet would be such as to place the Japanese in the most advantageous position to effect the destruction of the U.S. Fleet elements that were bound to sortie once news of Midway's fall reached Hawaii. The very large number of vessels employed in this operation, coupled with the need to ensure surprise, led to a wide dispersal of the forces involved.

The plan made provision for the assault on Midway to be initiated by Admiral Nagumo's First Carrier Air Fleet on 5 June, N minus 2. Approaching from the northwest, his four carriers were to launch their aircraft some 250 miles from Midway and then proceed to attack the atoll base, eliminating enemy air power on the island and softening up the defenses in readiness for the landings. Having fulfilled this task, Nagumo's carriers would then be free to tackle the U.S. carriers and other vessels it was presumed would sortie from Pearl Harbor following the fall of Midway. Provision of air support for the actual landings on 7 June was to be provided by "Rufe" floatplane fighters of Rear Admiral Fujita's Seaplane Tender Group who, on N minus 1, would seize the island of Kure barely 60 miles from Midway as a forward operating base. This was but the prelude to the amphibious landings to be made at dawn on 7 June by the Midway Invasion Force, which was coming up on the island from the south and carrying the army's only contribution to the offensive, in the form of the Ichicki detachment. The plan allowed for the discovery by the Americans of Tanaka's invasion force on 6 June (D–1), so that they would be led to believe that the main Japanese attack was coming from the south. The landings on Sand Island and Eastern Island would be given close support by the 8in gun batteries of Vice Admiral Kurita's four heavy cruisers. Lying further to the south and protecting the flank of the invasion force would be Kondo's Main Body.

By N-Day Admiral Yamamoto's Main Body, comprising the Combined Fleet's most powerful battleships and including the flagship *Yamato* (and

of whose presence the U.S. Navy was unaware until after the battle), would lie some 500 miles to the northwest of the island, along with other fleet elements already mentioned, ready to initiate the most important phase of Operation MI. This would occur when long-range air reconnaissance and the two submarine cordons stationed between Hawaii and Midway, planned to be on station on 2 June, informed Yamamoto that the U.S. Fleet had sortied from Pearl. Rapidly concentrating his widely dispersed forces Yamamoto would then force the "decisive battle" on the U.S. Fleet, from which the Japanese had no doubt they would emerge victorious, the *coup de grâce* being delivered by the heavy guns of the battleships. There were those among the Japanese, however, who expressed concern over the very tight timetable imposed on Nagumo's carriers. They believed that it placed a potentially dead hand on his freedom of movement by requiring him to reconcile two opposing objectives: destruction of Midway's air power and the defeat of the U.S.

▶ *The flagship of Nagumo's First Air Fleet for Operation MI was the venerable* Akagi *("Red Castle"). Originally designed as an* Amagi-*class battlecruiser she was converted following the Washington Naval Treaty to an aircraft carrier. She was launched in April 1925 with three flight decks forward. (via Roger Chesneau)*

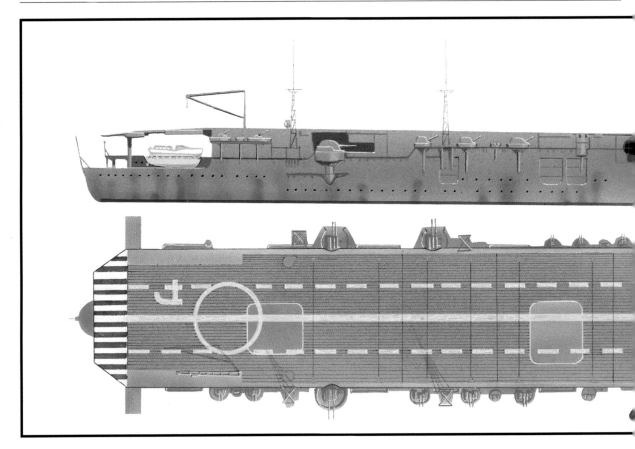

carriers, thus severely limiting his ability to respond in the face of an unexpected contingency. However, this was a minority view, and the prevailing sentiment was that all would be well, provided the U.S. Navy responded exactly as the Japanese predicted.

### A Profound Failure of Intelligence

Given the poverty of Combined Fleet's knowledge of the whereabouts of the U.S. Pacific Fleet, the presumed certainty of its position and reaction contained within this rigid plan is quite remarkable. In the end it was to prove to be its undoing. Indeed, the last reliable sighting of U.S. warships had occurred as far back as 18 May, when a number were spotted from the air to the east of the Solomon Islands. The estimate of U.S. strength that Yamamoto had issued on 20 May, covering the Aleutians, Hawaii and Midway, although not accurate, did draw attention to the strength of the Midway defenses, reinforcing the necessity for heavy air attacks to be launched on 5 June from Nagumo's carriers. He estimated the strength of U.S. Fleet assets in the Hawaii area as

two or three carriers, two or three escort carriers, four or five heavy cruisers, three or four light cruisers and about 30 destroyers and 25 submarines.

To illustrate the paucity of real knowledge of the position of the U.S. Fleet, the Naval General Staff in Tokyo was of the opinion that a U.S. Carrier Task Force was operating far to the south in the Solomons, providing evidence to their mind that the Americans were unaware of Japanese intentions. Yamamoto's own attempts to acquire more definitive intelligence about the shipping at Pearl came to nought when planned overflights of the Harbor by two Kawanishi H8K "Emily" flying boats between 31 May and 3 June were canceled because submarine I-123 reported that U.S. ships were patrolling their designated midflight refueling stop at the French Frigate Shoals. Nor did the submarine cordons have better luck. By the time they came on station, which was two days later than the planned D minus 5, Spruance had already passed by some days before, and *Yorktown* slipped through the cordon without detection.

Nevertheless, the Japanese did have indications that all might not be as they believed. On 1 June

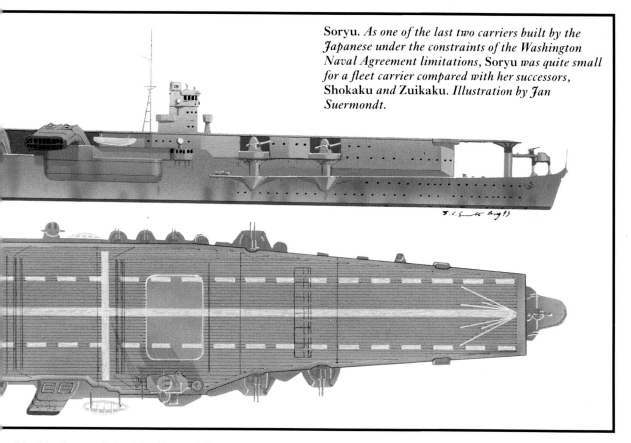

**Soryu.** *As one of the last two carriers built by the Japanese under the constraints of the Washington Naval Agreement limitations, Soryu was quite small for a fleet carrier compared with her successors,* **Shokaku** *and* **Zuikaku.** *Illustration by Jan Suermondt.*

Ugaki observed in his diary: "Out of 180 radio exchanges observed in the Hawaii district, as many as seventy-two were tagged 'urgent.' We believe that the enemy are preparing to meet us, after having strongly suspected our movement." This vital information was denied to Nagumo by the erroneous belief of those on board *Yamato* that this radio traffic must surely have been picked up on *Akagi*, and that Nagumo would, in consequence, take appropriate action. (This position was adhered to in spite of their knowledge that *Akagi*'s radio facilities were deficient. As it was, the American radio traffic was not picked up on the *Akagi*.) On this presumption it was argued there was no need to break the blanket radio silence Yamamoto had imposed upon the operation before the landings. For that same reason an updated and highly revealing message sent by the Naval General Staff on 2 June, speculating about the possible presence of a U.S. carrier force in the eastern Midway area lying in wait to ambush the advancing Japanese, was not passed on to Nagumo. Deprived of the information that could have significantly changed the outcome

of the events now about to unfold, Nagumo continued to plunge toward Midway, in possession of an intelligence picture almost as impenetrable as the fog banks through which his carriers were now moving.

### The American Plan

The plan that Nimitz presented to Spruance and Fletcher on 27 May had been formulated on the presumed accuracy of the most up-to-date intelligence picture of Japanese intentions and dispositions. Nimitz had already decided that the Aleutian operation was a diversion, but had nevertheless dispatched Task Force 8 under Rear Admiral Theobald to the Aleutians with five cruisers and ten destroyers – the most he could spare.

Midway figured prominently in Nimitz's planning by functioning as a fourth, unsinkable, aircraft carrier. While total airpower on the island was raised to 115 aircraft of differing types, by 3 June Nimitz was fully aware that the relative obsolescence of many of these precluded any possibility of prevent-

# JAPANESE ORDER OF BATTLE FOR OPERATIONS AL AND MI

## COMBINED FLEET
Admiral Isoroku Yamamoto in Fleet Flagship *Yamato*.

## OPERATION AL

### (A) NORTHERN (Aleutians) FORCE (Fifth Fleet):
Vice Admiral Moshiro Hosogaya in CA *Nachi*.
**Main Body:** Vice Admiral Moshiro Hosogaya in CA *Nachi*.
Screening Force: DD Inazuma: Commander Hajime
Takeuchi DD *Ikazuchi*.
Supply Group: 2 Oilers, 3 Cargo Ships.

### (B) SECOND CARRIER STRIKING FORCE:
Rear Admiral Kakuji Kakuta.
CARRIER GROUP (CARDIV 4): Rear Admiral Kakuji
Kakuta.
CVL *Ryujo*: Captain Tadeo Kato.
Air Unit: Lt Masayuki Yamagami.
Air Component: 16 Zero A6M2 Type 21: Lt Koboyashi.
21 B5N2: Lt Yamagami.
CV *Junyo*: Captain Shizue Isii.
Air Unit: Lt Yoshio Shiga.
Air Component: 24 Zero A6M2 Type 21: Lt Shiga.
21 D3A1: Lt Abe.
Support Group: 2nd Section CruDiv 4: Capt Shunsaku
Nabeshima in CA *Maya*.
CA *Takao*.
Screening Group: DesDiv 7: Capt Kaname Konishi.
3 DDs: *Akebono, Ushio, Sazanami.*.
1 Oiler.

### (C) ALEUTIAN SUPPORT FORCE:
Vice Admiral Shiro Takasu in BB *Hyuga* (flagship).
Battleship Group: *Hyuga, Ise, Fuso, Yamashiro*.
Screening Force: CruDiv 9: CL *Kitikami* (flagship), CL *Oi*.
DesDiv 20: 4 DDs: *Asagiri, Yugiri, Shirakumo, Amagiri*.
DesDiv 24: 4 DDs: *Umikaze, Yamakaze, Kawakaze,
Suzukaze*.
DesDiv 27: 4 DDs: *Ariake, Yugure, Shigure, Shiratsuyu*.
Supply Group: 2 Oilers.

### (D) ATTU INVASION FORCE:
Rear Admiral Sentaro Omori in CL *Abukuma*.
DesDiv 21: 4 DDs: *Wakaba, Nenohi, Hatsuharu, Hatsushimo*.
1 Minelayer.
1 Transport.

### (E) KISKA INVASION FORCE:
Captain Takeji Ono in CL *Kiso*.
CruDiv 21: 2 CLs: *Kiso, Tama*.
1 Auxiliary Cruiser.
Screening Force: DesDiv 6: 3 DDs: *Hibiki, Akatsuki, Hokaze*.
Transports: *Hakusan Maru* (carrying 550 troops), *Kumagawa
Maru*.
Minesweeper Div 13: 3 Minesweepers
Submarine Detachment: 6 Submarines: *I-9, I-15, I-17, I-19,
I-25, I-26*.

## OPERATION MI

### (F) MAIN FORCE (FIRST FLEET):
Admiral Isoroku Yamamoto in BB *Yamato*.
Main Body: Admiral Yamamoto.
Battleship Group: BatDiv 1: Admiral Yamamoto in *Yamato,
Nagato, Mutsu*.
Carrier Group: *Hosho* carrying 8 B5N1 and B5N2.
DD *Yukaze*.
Special Force: *Chiyoda, Nisshin* (although seaplane carriers,
these two vessels carried only midget submarines for this
operation).
Screening Force: DesRon 3: Rear Admiral Shintaro
Hashimoto in CL *Sendai* (Flagship).
DesDiv 11: 4 DDs: *Fubuki, Shirayuki, Hatsuyuki, Murakamo*.
DesDiv 19: 4 DDs: *Isonami, Uranami, Shikinami, Ayanami*.
Supply Group: 2 Oilers.

### (G) FIRST CARRIER STRIKING FORCE:
(First Air Fleet) Vice Admiral Nagumo.
Carrier Division (CarDiv 1): Vice Admiral Nagumo in CV
*Akagi*.
*Akagi* (CV): Captain Taijiro Aoki.
Air Unit: Commander Mitsuo Fuchida.
Air Component: 21 Zero A6M2 type 21: Lt Commander
Itaya.
21 D3A1: Lt Commander Chihaya.
21 B5N2: Lt Commander Murata.
*Kaga* (CV): Captain Jisaku Okada.
Air Unit: Lt Commander Tadashi Kusumi
Air Component: 21 Zero A6M2 Type 21: Lt Sato.
21 D3A1: Lt Ogawa.
30 B5N2s: Lt Kitajima.
Carrier Division 2 (CarDiv 2): Rear Admiral Tamon
Yamaguchi in CV *Hiryu*.
*Hiryu* (CV): Captain Tomeo Kaku.
Air Unit: Lt Joichi Tomonaga.
Air Component: 21 Zero A6M2 Type 21: Lt Mori.
21 D3A1: Lt Kobayashi.
21 B5N2: Lt Kikuchi
*Soryu* (CV): Captain Ryusaku Yanagimoto
Air Unit: Lt Commander Takashige Egusa.
Air Component: 21 A6M2 Zero Type 21: Lt Suganami.
21 D3A1: Lt Ikeda.
21 B5N2: Lt Abe.
2 D4Y1.
Support Group: Rear Admiral Hiroaki Abe in CA *Tone*.
CRUDIV 8: Rear Admiral Abe.
CA *Tone* and CA *Chikuma*.
2ND SECTION, BATDIV3: BB *Haruna*, BB *Kirishima*.
Screening Force: DesRon 10: Rear Admiral Kimura in CL
*Nagara*.
DesDiv 4: 4 DDs: *Nowaki, Arashi, Hagikaze, Maikaze*.

DesDiv 10: 3 DDs: *Kazagumo, Yugomo, Makigumo.*
DesDiv 17: 4 DDs: *Urakaze, Isokaze, Tanikaze, Hamakaze.*
Supply Group: 1 DD: *Akigumo.*
5 Oilers.

## MIDWAY INVASION FORCE (SECOND FLEET):
Vice Admiral Nobutake in CA *Atago.*

## (H) SECOND FLEET MAIN BODY:
Vice Admiral Kondo.
CRUDIV 4 (less 2nd Section): CA *Atago*, CA *Chokai.*
CRUDIV 5: CA *Myoko*, CA *Haguro.*
BATDIV 3 (less 2nd Section): BB *Kongo*, BB *Hiei.*
Screening Force: DesRon 4: Rear Admiral Nishimura in CL *Yura.*
DesDiv 2: 4 DDs: *Murusame, Samidare, Harusame, Yudachi.*
DesDiv 9: 3 DDs: *Asagumo, Minegumo, Natsugumo.*
Carrier Group: Captain Sueo Obayashi
*Zuiho:* Captain Obayashi.
Air Component: 12 A6M2 Zero Type 21: Lt Hidaka.
12 B5N2: Lt Matsuo.
1 DD: *Mikazuki.*
Supply Group: 4 Oilers.
1 Repair ship.

## MIDWAY OCCUPATION FORCE:
Rear Admiral Raizo Tanaka.
12 Transport vessels.
3 Patrol Boats.
(These vessels were carrying approx 5,000 troops. Capt Ota (Navy) commanded the 2nd Special Naval Landing Force and the Army detachment under Col Kiyonao Ichiki.)
1 Oiler.
Escort Force: Rear Admiral Tanaka in CL *Jintsu.*
DesDiv 15: 2 DDs: *Kuroshio, Oyashio.*
DesDiv 16: 4 DDs: *Yukikaze, Amatsukaze, Tokitsukaze, Hatsukaze.*
DesDiv 18: 4 DDs: *Shiranuhi, Kasumi, Arare, Kagero.*
Seaplane Tender Group: Rear Admiral Ruitaro Fujita in CVS *Chitose.*
Seaplane Tender Div II: CVS *Chitose.*
Air Component: 16 A6M2-N "Rufe" floatplane fighters.
4 scout airplanes.
AV *Kamikawa Maru.*
8 A6M-2N "Rufe" floatplane fighters.
4 scout airplanes.
1 DD *Hayashio.*
1 Patrol boat.

## (J) MIDWAY SUPPORT FORCE:
Vice Admiral Takeo Kurita in CA *Kumano.*
CRUDIV 7: Vice Admiral Kurita.
4 CAs: *Kumano, Suzuya, Mogami, Mikuma.*
DesDiv 8: 2 DDs: *Asashio, Arashio.*
1 Oiler.

## (K) MINESWEEPER GROUP:
Capt Sadatomo Miyamoto.
4 Minesweepers.
3 Subchasers.
1 Supply ship.
2 Cargo ships.

## ADVANCE (Submarine) FORCE (Sixth Fleet):
Vice Admiral Teruhisa Komatsu, in *Katori* at Kwajalein.
SubRon 3: Rear Admiral Chimaki Kono
Rio de Janeiro (flagship at Kwajalein)
(L & M) SUBDIV 19: Capt Ryojiro Ono
*I-156, I-157, I-158, I-159.*
SUBDIV 30: Capt Maseo Teraoka
*I-162, I-165, I-166.*
SUBDIV 13: Capt Takeharu Miyazaki
*I-121, I-122, I-123.*

## SHORE BASED AIR FORCE (Eleventh Air Fleet):
Vice Admiral Nishizo Tsukahara (at Tinian)
Midway Expeditionary Force: Capt Morita
36 "Zero" fighters.
10 "Betty" bombers at Wake.
6 flying boats at Jaluit.
24th Air Flotilla: Rear Admiral Maeda
Chitose Air Group at Kwajalein
36 "Zero" fighters.
36 B5N2s.
1st Air Group at Aur and Wotje
36 "Zero" fighters.
36 B5N2s.
14th Air Group
36 H6K Flying boats at Jaluit and Wotje.

ing repeated raids on the atoll base by Nagumo's aircraft. Under such circumstances he recognized that the only way Midway could maximize the limited capabilities of the airpower it possessed would be to "inflict prompt and early damage to Jap carrier flight decks," in the hope of catching their aircraft before they took off. He therefore instructed the air commander that the fighters on Midway should be employed to escort the bombers and not to defend the airbase. That task should be left to the antiaircraft guns. He also expected that the long-range air patrols flown by PBY-5As from the island,

## U.S. FORCES ORDER OF BATTLE FOR THE MIDWAY CAMPAIGN

**U.S. PACIFIC FLEET AND PACIFIC OCEAN AREAS**
Admiral Chester W. Nimitz

**CARRIER STRIKING FORCE:**
Rear Admiral Frank Fletcher

**Task Force 17:** Rear Admiral Frank Fletcher.
TG 17.5 Carrier Group: Capt Elliot Buckmaster.
*Yorktown* (CV): Capt Elliot Buckmaster.
Air Component: VF-3: 25 F4F-4 Wildcat.
VB-3: 18 SBD-3 Dauntless.
VS-3: 19 SBD-3 Dauntless.
VT-3: 13 TBD-1 Devastator.
TG 17.2 Cruiser Group: Rear Admiral William Smith in CA *Astoria*.
CA *Astoria*, CA *Portland*.
TG 17.4 Destroyer Group: Capt Gilbert C. Hoover (ComDesRon 2).

6 DDs: *Hamman, Hughes, Morris, Anderson, Russell, Gwin.*

**Task Force 16:** Rear Admiral Raymond Spruance.
TG 16.5 Carrier Group: Capt George D. Murray.
*Enterprise* (CV): Capt George D. Murray.
Air Component: VF-6: 27 F4F-4 Wildcats.
VB-6: 19 SBD-2 & 3 Dauntless.
VS-6: 19 SBD-2 & 3 Dauntless.
VT-6: 14 TBD-1 Devastator.
*Hornet* (CV): Captain Marc A. Mitscher.
Air Component: VF-8: 27 F4F-4 Wildcat.
VB-8: 19 SBD-2 & 3 Dauntless.
VS-8: 19 SBD-1, 2 & 3 Dauntless.
VT-8: 15 TBD-1 Devastator.
TG 16.2 Cruiser Group: Rear Admiral Thomas C. Kinkaid (ComCruDiv 6).
CA *New Orleans*, CA *Minneapolis*.
TG 16.4 Dest Screen: Capt Alexander R. Early (ComDesRon 1).

beginning as early as 22 May, would serve as the eyes of Midway and of the Carrier Task Forces, and that first contact with the approaching Japanese forces would be made by them.

However, with the exception of Shannon, Simard and a few other higher ranks, Nimitz had not revealed that the efforts of the defending Midway forces would be supported by the Navy's carriers. There was no attempt to coordinate the efforts of Army, Navy and Marine air units on Midway itself,

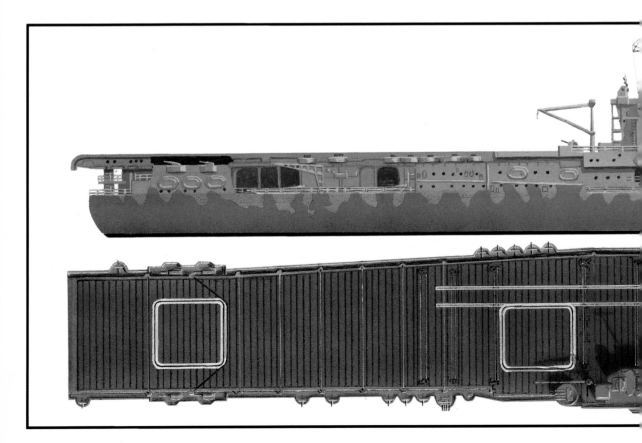

9 DDs: *Phelps, Worden, Monaghan, Aylwin, Balch, Conyngham, Benham, Ellet, Maury.*
Oiler Group: *Cimmarron, Platte.*
2 DDs: *Dewey, Monssen.*

## SUBMARINES
Rear Admiral Robert H. English, Comm Sub Force, Pacific Fleet at Pearl Harbor (Operational Control).
TG 7.1: Midway Patrol Group 12 subs: *Cachalot, Flying Fish, Tambor, Trout, Grayling, Nautilus, Grouper, Dolphin, Gato, Cuttlefish, Gudgeon, Grenadier.*
TG 7.2: "Roving Short Stop" Group: 3 subs: *Narwhal, Plunger, Trigger.*
TG 7.3: North of Oahu Patrol Group: 4 subs: *Tarpon, Pike, Finback, Growler.*

## MIDWAY-BASED AIR
Capt Cyril T. Simard.
Detachments of Patrol Wings 1 & 2.
38 PBY-5 and PBY-5A Catalina.

VT-8 detachment: 6 TBF-1.
Marine Air Group 22, 2nd Marine Air Wing: Lt Ira L. Kimes.
VMF 221: 20 F2A-3 Buffalo, 7 F4F-3 Wildcat.
VMSB: 11 SB2U-3 Vindicator, 16 SBD Dauntless.
Detachment of 7th USAAF: Major Gen Willis P. Hale
4 B-26, 19 B-17E.

## MIDWAY LOCAL DEFENSES
6th Marine Defense Battalion.
Fleet Marine Force: Col Harold D. Shannon.
MTB Squadron 1.
8 PT Boats at Midway: 2 at Kure Island.
4 small patrol craft deployed in area.
2 tenders, 1 DD at French Frigate Shoals.
1 Oiler, 1 converted yacht.
1 minesweeper at Pearl and Hermes reef.
2 converted tuna boats at Lisianski, Gardner Pinnacles, Laysan and Necker.
Midway Relief Fueling Unit: 1 oiler, 2 DDs.

or to coordinate them with the Navy forces at sea. Indeed, Navy pilots on the island were told quite specifically that the carriers' first priority was to protect Pearl Harbor, inferring their absence from Midway's defense when the Japanese attacked. Nothing could be permitted that would in any way compromise the absolute secrecy of the presence of the carriers to the northeast of Midway Island, for Nimitz was depending on the aircraft spotted on their decks for a successful outcome in the days ahead. For

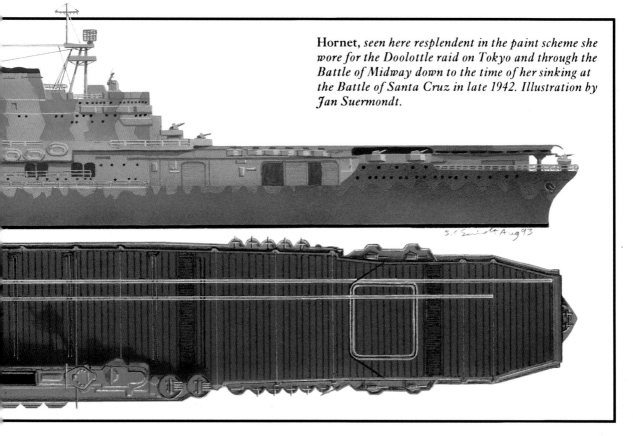

**Hornet,** *seen here resplendent in the paint scheme she wore for the Doolottle raid on Tokyo and through the Battle of Midway down to the time of her sinking at the Battle of Santa Cruz in late 1942. Illustration by Jan Suermondt.*

## Japanese Battleships in Operation MI

| Name | Displacement | Armament | Armor | Completed | Fate |
|------|-------------|----------|-------|-----------|------|
| *Yamato* | 72,800 tons | 9 x 18.1in<br>12 x 6.1in<br>12 x 5in AA | 400mm belt<br>500/650mm turrets<br>200mm decks | Dec 1941 | Sunk April 1945 |
| *Nagato* | 34,100 tons | 8 x 16in<br>18 x 5.5in<br>8 x 5in AA | 100/300mm belt | Nov 1920 | Expended 1946 in Bikini<br>Atoll bomb tests |
| *Mutsu* | 34,100 tons | 8 x 16in<br>18 x 5.5in<br>8 x 5in AA<br>4 x 533mm torpedo tubes. | 356mm turrets<br>Up to 75mm decks | Oct 1921 | Accidental internal<br>explosion, 1943 |
| *Kirishima* | 27,500 tons | 8 x 14in<br>14 x 6in<br>8 x 5in AA | 76/203mm belt | Apr 1915 | Sunk 1942 off Guadalcanal |
| *Haruna* | 27,500 tons | 8 x 14in<br>14 x 6in | 229mm turrets | Apr 1915 | Sunk July 1945 |

added security Nimitz pulled back some 19 submarines from their offensive duties, and for the duration of the battle allocated 16 of them the defensive task of screening Midway. Another four covered Oahu, leaving three available on call.

The principal target of U.S. action, however, was beyond dispute. It was Nagumo's four carriers, known to be approaching Midway from the northwest. Nimitz pronounced to Fletcher and Spruance that, in seeking their destruction, it was absolutely vital for the U.S. carriers to achieve surprise by hitting them first and from the flank.

The overwhelming Japanese material superiority over the U.S. Navy precluded any option other than a savage and devastating hit-and-run strike. Because surprise and speed were the essence of his plan, Nimitz had consciously eschewed the employment of the slow battleships of Task Force One based in San Francisco.

Given how few were the naval assets now possessed by the U.S. Navy in the Pacific, the option of a drawn-out battle of attrition was not a possibility. If Fletcher and Spruance failed and the U.S. carriers were sunk, the whole of the Pacific and the eastern seaboard of the United States would lay open to the Japanese. Nimitz could not fail to impress upon his subordinates that their actions, in the light of these facts, must be guided by "the principle of calculated risk." Fletcher and Spruance were to engage only if they had a good chance of inflicting disproportionate damage on the Japanese. Despite the remarkable intelligence provided by Hypo, Nimitz knew that the operation they had embarked upon was a very great gamble. A great deal could go wrong; certainly the battle was not in the bag. Little wonder, then, that he named the rendezvous point of the three U.S. carriers at 32 degrees north latitude, 173 degrees west longitude and 325 miles to the northeast of Midway "Point Luck."

# THE OPPOSING COMMANDERS

## Japanese Commanders

Admiral Isoroku Yamamoto emerges from any account of the Midway operation as the central and supreme moving force on the Japanese side. It has already been shown how this arose as a consequence of his dominance within the Combined Fleet and over the senior officers of the Naval General Staff. In reality the Midway plan was his, and when it failed and failed totally, he made no attempt to shift the blame to a convenient scapegoat. Postbattle analysis by the Japanese was to reveal a host of shortcomings regarding the operation, but strangely enough these seem never to have colored their own assessment of Admiral Yamamoto as a military commander of the first order.

Perhaps the key to the failure of Operation MI lies in the temperament of the Combined Fleet Commander. A patriot to his fingertips, he was nevertheless all too aware that Japan's Pacific War was, above all, a reckless gamble. As an inveterate gambler himself, whether at poker or *shogi*, he had perhaps persuaded himself that the only possibility for his homeland's survival lay in an operation in which everything had to be staked on one card. This might explain not only his almost pathological insistence on the speed with which MI was carried out, but also the reckless commitment of resources to the vast Midway enterprise without a detailed, up-to-the-minute intelligence appraisal of the strength and disposition of the U.S. Fleet. Without doubt, his unwillingness to brook any opposition to Operation MI was driven as much by his own awareness of America's inevitable recovery as it was by his very genuine sense of failure, perhaps even of personal dishonor, in having allowed the Emperor's person to have been threatened by the Doolittle Raid.

▶ *Admiral Isoroku Yamamoto, Commander in Chief of the Combined Fleet, architect of the Pearl Harbor attack and prime mover behind the calamitous Operation MI. Venerated by the officers and men of the Rengo Kantai, he could trace his career back to service with Admiral Togo at the battle of Tsushima in 1905. After Midway he continued to serve as Fleet Commander until his death on 18 April 1943 when he fell victim to a long-range aerial ambush staged by U.S. P-38 Lightning fighters while undertaking an inspection tour of South Sea bases. he was posthumously promoted to the rank of full Fleet Admiral. (U.S. National Archives)*

His great reputation, particularly in Japan, rests on the claim that he was a pioneer in the development of naval air power. While it is true that he did oversee a major expansion of this arm of the *Rengo Kantai*, there are more than a few pointers in the period between Pearl Harbor and the execution of Operation MI to suggest that, at a more fundamental level, he had not grasped the full implications of the truly radical change that air power had wrought on naval warfare. This can perhaps be inferred from his readiness to comply with the "breaking up" of the First Air Fleet following the Pearl Harbor attack, as if he were unaware of the revolutionary nature of that unique formation. It is also implicit in the highly convoluted nature of the plan for Operation MI, which turned on the denouement of the U.S. Pacific Fleet in the *Kantai Kessen*, wherein the ruin of American warships would be brought about not by the aircraft of Nagumo's carriers, but by the 16in and 18in guns of Yamamoto's inappropriately named "Main Body" of battleships. Clearly, the carriers were seen to have a vital role, but as understudies to the battlewagons.

Additionally, the dispersion of the very large number of warships assembled for MI, while ostensibly serving the need for surprise and security, actually contributed to the very dissipation of the mass required for the decisive battle. Vital assets like the carriers *Ryujo* and *Junyo* were wasted in the diversionary Aleutians operation which failed totally in its purpose. The dispersion also deprived Nagumo's carriers of the myriad antiaircraft batteries aboard the many cruisers and battleships that would have greatly assisted the flattops in fighting off the U.S. air attacks. Such a proposal, to reorganize the Combined Fleet around three carrier groups in a manner analogous to the U.S. Navy Task Forces, was argued for by Vice Admiral Tamon Yamaguchi in the wake of the Coral Sea Battle, but was not acted upon in time for Midway. To have acceded to this position would have marked the final subservience of the battleship to naval air power in the *Rengo Kantai*. However, it was to take the shattering defeat at Midway for the big-gun capital ship advocates to accept that change. Comment has also often been made on the dead hand

*Far left: Vice Admiral Chuichi Nagumo commanded the First Air Fleet at Pearl Harbor and at Midway. A man out of place in Naval Aviation, of which he knew virtually nothing, he has been castigated for command failures in both operations. After Midway he continued to command carriers, but was dismissed after the Battle of Santa Cruz in October 1942. As commander of the forces on Saipan he committed suicide when the island was overrun by U.S. forces in 1944. (U.S. National Archives)*

*Left: Admiral Osami Nagano, who, as Chief of the Naval General Staff, sanctioned Yamamoto's plans for the Pearl Harbor attack and the Midway operation. On both occasions his decision was encouraged by Yamamoto's threat to resign as Fleet Commander unless his plans for both operations were endorsed.*

*Right: Rear Admiral Tamon Yamaguchi was one of the most airminded of Japanese admirals. Like Yamamoto, Yamaguchi had served as naval attache in Washington, and had attended Princeton University. Highly regarded by the Fleet Commander he took command of the Second Carrier Division in November 1940 and led it in the attacks on Pearl Harbor and at Midway where he chose to go down with his flagship, the carrier* Hiryu, *at Midway on 5 June.*

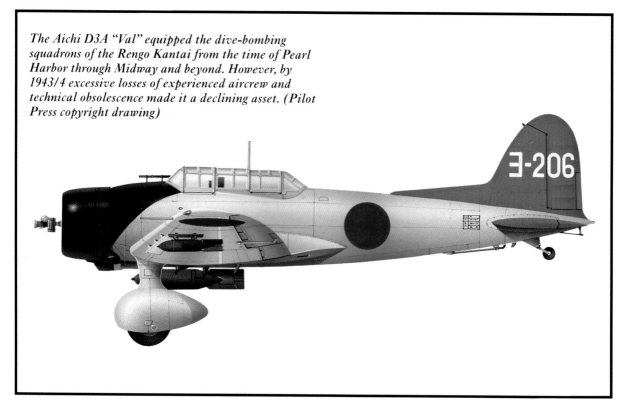

*The Aichi D3A "Val" equipped the dive-bombing squadrons of the Rengo Kantai from the time of Pearl Harbor through Midway and beyond. However, by 1943/4 excessive losses of experienced aircrew and technical obsolescence made it a declining asset. (Pilot Press copyright drawing)*

placed on MI, once it had begun, by Yamamoto's anachronistic decision to go to sea himself. He should have stayed at Hashirajima, as Nimitz did at Oahu, so that he could marshal and command his forces in response to intelligence. Once at sea, as we shall observe shortly, the very radio silence he imposed on the fleet to ensure tactical surprise was also imposed on himself, totally negating any value in his presence at sea.

Much more questionable, particularly when it was within his power to do something about it, was Yamamoto's continued retention of Vice Admiral Chuichi Nagumo as commander of the First Air Fleet. There can be no doubting the excellent service record of this torpedo specialist who had commanded cruisers and battleships, but his appointment to command this formation was a most unlikely choice, given his complete lack of experience with naval air power. Indeed, it was said of him by a close service colleague that he had no real conception of the power or potentialities of the naval air arm. His appointment was not by design, but was the consequence of seniority and protocol which required his filling the post when it fell vacant. Although Yamamoto expressed a degree of unhappiness about Nagumo's performance at Pearl Harbor, he was not prepared to replace him because it is said that he feared Nagumo would take his loss of command as a personal dishonor and commit suicide.

Nonetheless, Nagumo was undoubtedly the most successful carrier admiral in the world at the time of the Midway battle. Besides Pearl Harbor, Nagumo's carriers had rampaged through the south seas and the Indian Ocean, and the sense of invincibility engendered by these victories certainly put Nagumo in a most optimistic state of mind on the eve of Midway. Even so, he was to make a number of major errors in the battle, such as the inadequate air search procedures that, in hindsight, were not insignificant in bringing about the Japanese defeat, even though such decisions appeared both logical and sound at the time.

## United States Commanders

There is a real sense in which the main U.S. commanders in the battle revealed a degree of profes-

sional realism and objectivity that sets them apart from their Japanese counterparts. Without doubt the most remarkable was Fleet Admiral Chester Nimitz. Once he had taken on the mantle of Commander in Chief Pacific Fleet, his personable style of man management rapidly raised morale in the wake of Pearl Harbor. The preparation for Midway showed his remarkable gift for trusting colleagues to employ their expertise and then to act upon their ideas when he was convinced they were right. In particular, his willingness to take seriously the views and judgments of Commander Rochefort, and to trust them even when his own superior, Admiral King, did not, was absolutely crucial. His deployment of his limited naval assets was based on his conviction that Rochefort's intelligence was accurate. Admiral King certainly fretted over Nimitz's judgments concerning Japan's likely

*Left: Chester William Nimitz was appointed Commander in Chief of the U.S. Pacific Fleet (CINCPAC) on 31 December 1941, taking over from the dismissed Admiral Kimmel. Within weeks of his appointment he had transformed morale in the fleet. His decision to act on the intelligence provided by Hypo, and in consequence garner his limited naval assets and employ them to defeat Nagumo's carriers, made him the real architect of the American victory. Following Midway* he became Commander in Chief Central Pacific Area, wherein he shared responsibility with Douglas MacArthur for prosecution of the Pacific War. In 1944 he was promoted to Fleet Admiral, and in September 1945 he was among the Allied team that accepted the Japanese surrender aboard the USS Missouri *in Tokyo Bay. (U.S. National Archives)*

*Above: Rear Admiral Frank "Blackjack" Fletcher was the commander of the U.S. naval* forces at the Coral Sea, and of Task Forces 16 and 17 during the Battle of Midway. Although victor in both battles, he was regarded as an overly cautious carrier commander, illustrated by his handling of the battles around Guadalcanal in August 1942, which was regarded as lackluster. (U.S. National Archives)*

*Right: When appointed to replace the unwell Halsey as commander of Task Force 16, Rear Admiral Raymond A. Spruance had no experi-* ence as a carrier commander. However, he had a remarkably flexible and adaptable intellect and incisive but balanced judgment, which made his appointment most apposite for the particular conditions of Midway. He was in many senses the "right man for the right job." Although unknown to the Japanese before the battle, he was to establish himself from June 1942 onward as one of the foremost commanders of U.S. Naval forces in the Pacific War. (U.S. National Archives)*

intentions before Midway. He was acutely aware that his Pacific admiral was in a position analogous to that of Jellicoe at Jutland, as being the "only man who could lose the war in an afternoon." However, the fate of the U.S. Navy could not have been in better hands.

Chester Nimitz never ceased to pay tribute to the crucial role played in the battle by Rear Admiral Raymond Spruance, frequently stating that it was he who was really responsible for the victory at Midway. Given that Spruance was not a carrier admiral and had only been drafted in at the last moment because of "Bull" Halsey's dermatitis, this is high praise indeed. Some have rated Spruance's appointment as Nimitz's most important command decision of the battle. While he never denigrated Halsey's own particular leadership skills, Nimitz insisted that Spruance's analytical intellect and calm and collective disposition made him absolutely right for the peculiar conditions of the Midway battle. In later years Nimitz, reflecting upon the happy role played by fate in causing Spruance to be appointed to the command of Task Force 16, said: "It was a great day for the Navy when Bill Halsey had to enter the hospital." Although he always consciously eschewed the publicity that Halsey loved, Spruance

generated a reputation that, in the end, was totally grounded on his professionalism. However, he was never in any doubt as to where the credit for Midway lay. He laid it firmly at the feet of Nimitz as the one who had the courage to accept the intelligence picture and act upon it.

Although Admiral Frank Fletcher played a crucial part in the victory of Midway, he tends to stand in the shadows of his nominal subordinate Raymond Spruance and his superior Admiral Nimitz. His performance in the Coral Sea exposed him to criticism, but he incorporated his experiences of that battle into his tactics at Midway. Of particular importance was his decision to separate the two Task Groups, so that they would not provide the Japanese with one target had all three carriers operated in close proximity.

The consequences of operating thus were to become abundantly clear to the Japanese before very long. Furthermore, letting Spruance lead off against the Japanese carriers on 4 June inevitably meant that he would acquire the kudos for delivering the first blow. That he knowingly sacrificed this personal prestige for the sake of operational effectiveness has been held by many to be the measure of the man.

*The courageous fight put up by US Marine pilots in Brewster F2 Buffaloes – obsolescent by the time of Midway – caused many Japanese flyers bombing the atoll base to misidentify them as Wildcats. (Pilot Press copyright drawing)*

# THE OPPOSING
# NAVAL AIR ARMS

### The Japanese

The most visible and potent symbol of Japanese military prowess in the first six months of the Pacific War was the Mitsubishi A6M2 "Zero-Sen" carrier fighter. This was a remarkable compromise of a clean lightweight airframe conveying great manœuvrability allied to very long-range and heavy firepower. Ever since Pearl Harbor the "Zero" had swept Allied airpower from the skies wherever it had been encountered, generating a reputation that, by the time of Midway, verged on the mythical. Only after recovering an almost intact example that had crashed in the Aleutians during Operation AL were the Americans able to define the Achilles' heel of this outstanding aircraft. Nevertheless, it was the air

superiority gained by this fighter, flown by highly skilled and experienced aircrew such as Lieutenant Commander Shigeru Itaya of the *Akagi*, that had enabled the dive-bomber and torpedo-bomber squadrons of the *Rengo Kantai* to employ their fearful expertise against Allied sea and land targets.

In the Aichi D3A1 "Val" dive bomber the Japan-

▼ *Although demonstrating great effectiveness in the Battle of Midway the repeated low-level attacks by the TBDs pulled the Zero Combat Air Patrol over Nagumo's fleet down from height to sea level. This left the skies above* *the Japanese carriers naked and free for the Dauntless dive-bombers to deliver their devastating strikes without fear of interception by these potent Japanese fighters. (Philip Jarrett)*

## Japanese Aircraft Carriers at Midway

| Name | Displacement | Length | Armament |
|---|---|---|---|
| Akagi | 36,500 tons | 885ft | Six 8-inch guns<br>Twelve 4.7inch guns<br>28 25mm AA<br>63 aircraft |
| Kaga | 38,200 tons | 812ft | Ten 20cm MG<br>Eight 12.7cm AA<br>72 aircraft |
| Soryu | 18,800 tons | 746ft | Twelve 12.7cm AA<br>26 25mm AA guns<br>63 aircraft |
| Hiryu | 17,300 tons | 746ft | Twelve 12.7cm AA<br>34 25mm AA<br>63 aircraft |

Aircraft numbers reflect those actually carried in the Midway attack, rather than total possible number of airplanes that could be carried; i.e. Kaga could carry maximum of 90 aircraft.

ese possessed an effective design which, in the hands of expert pilots, had realized a strike accuracy of 80 percent against Royal Navy warships during the rampage across the Indian Ocean in April 1942. Although it was a large machine with a fixed spatted undercarriage, the "Val" had demonstrated a remarkable capacity for dogfighting in the Battle of the Coral Sea. Two examples of the D3A1A's replacement, the Yokosuka D4Y1 "Judy," were present at Midway aboard the carrier *Soryu* for employment as reconnaissance aircraft. The Nakajima B5N2 "Kate," of which 93 equipped the torpedo bombing squadrons of Nagumo's carriers in June

▼ **Akagi** *was extensively rebuilt between 1936 and 1938 and modernized with a full length single flight deck. Her last significant modification was the replacement in the late 1930s of her 270ft funnel by a large single stack canted downward to vent the fumes away from the flight deck as illustrated here. She appeared thus at Midway.*

## U.S. and Japanese Fighter Aircraft at Midway

| Country | Type | Armament | Engine | Max Speed | Range | Ceiling | Span | Length |
|---|---|---|---|---|---|---|---|---|
| USA | Grumman F4F-4 Wildcat | 6 x 0.50in MG | 1,200hp R-1830-86 | 318mph | 900 miles | 35,000ft | 38ft 0in | 28ft 9in |
| USA | Brewster F2A Buffalo | 4 x 0.50in MG | 1,100hp | 300mph | 950 miles | 30,500ft | 35ft 0in | 26ft 4in |
| Japan | Mitsubishi Type 21 A6M-2 Zero | 2 x 20mm Type 99 cannon + 2 x 7.7mm Type 97 MG | 925hp Sakae 12 | 316mph | 1,940 miles | 33,790ft | 39ft 4½in | 29ft 9in |

## Japanese Battleships in Operation MI

| Name | Displacement | Armament | Armor | Completed | Fate |
|------|-------------|----------|-------|-----------|------|
| Yamato | 72,800 tons | 9 x 18.1in<br>12 x 6.1in<br>12 x 5in AA | 400mm belt<br>500/650mm turrets<br>200mm decks | Dec 1941 | Sunk April 1945 |
| Nagato | 34,100 tons | 8 x 16in<br>18 x 5.5in<br>8 x 5in AA | 100/300mm belt | Nov 1920 | Expended 1946 in Bikini Atoll bomb tests |
| Mutsu | 34,100 tons | 8 x 16in<br>18 x 5.5in<br>8 x 5in AA<br>4 x 533mm torpedo tubes. | 356mm turrets<br>Up to 75mm decks | Oct 1921 | Accidental internal explosion, 1943 |
| Kirishima | 27,500 tons | 8 x 14in<br>14 x 6in<br>8 x 5in AA | 76/203mm belt | Apr 1915 | Sunk 1942 off Guadalcanal |
| Haruna | 27,500 tons | 8 x 14in<br>14 x 6in | 229mm turrets | Apr 1915 | Sunk July 1945 |

1942, was the best aircraft of its type in the world, outmatching its American and British equivalents. However, its superior performance was only relative, for like all aircraft of its type its large size, slow speed and poor armament made it vulnerable to fighter attack and antiaircraft fire. Nevertheless, its achievements during the period to Midway had been remarkable. It was also employed in the level-bombing role in the attack on Midway Island, as well as in its principal role of torpedo bomber in the attacks on the U.S. carriers.

In spite of the technical proficiency of its aircraft, by the time of Midway a major problem had begun to emerge for the Japanese Naval Air Arm which was undoubtedly to have an influence on the outcome of the battle and was to handicap them dramatically throughout the rest of the war. Unlike most of the battleships of the Combined Fleet, which had resided in majestic splendor at the Hashirajima anchorage since the outbreak of war, the carriers of the First Air Fleet had been in almost continual action since Pearl Harbor. As a result, the inevitable attrition had begun to make dangerous inroads into aircrew numbers. The Japanese Navy had entered the war with a fairly small pool of 5,000 pilots, of whom some 3,500 were serving front-line flyers. Owing to the policy of retaining the *experten* in front-line squadrons to ensure a qualitative advantage in combat, very few of these veterans survived to pass on their expertise to the new replacement aircrew training in Japan. Thus most, if not all, replacement aircrew were rank novices needing a

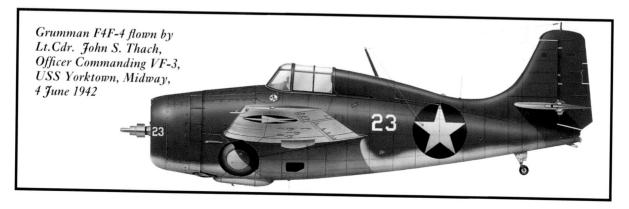

*Grumman F4F-4 flown by Lt.Cdr. John S. Thach, Officer Commanding VF-3, USS Yorktown, Midway, 4 June 1942*

## U.S. Aircraft Carriers at Midway

As *Hornet*, *Enterprise* and *Yorktown* were of the same class, the following information is generally applicable to all three vessels.

| | |
|---|---|
| Standard displacement: | 19,800 tons |
| Overall length: | 809$\frac{1}{2}$ft |
| Aircraft complement: | 85-100 |
| Armament (1942): | eight 5in 38 cal AA guns (single mounts) |
| | sixteen 1.1in MG AA (4 quad mounts) |
| | 23 x 20mm MG (single mounts) |
| Date of completion: | 20 October 1941 |

great deal of time and effort to work up to even minimal combat efficiency.

The fallacy of this policy became apparent after the Coral Sea, when the losses of irreplaceable veteran aircrew such as Lieutenant Commander Takahashi, who had led the dive-bombers at Pearl Harbor, resulted in the new fleet carrier *Zuikaku* being withdrawn from Operation MI because of a lack of trained aircrew. Indeed, Nagumo was to comment unfavorably on the poor quality of many of the replacement crews despatched to serve on the carriers. As we shall see, the growing crisis in the supply of aircrew was only compounded for the Japanese by the grievous losses they were to sustain among the remaining veteran aircrew at Midway.

### The Americans

In the coming battle, which would be waged by aircraft against each other and by aircraft against warships, the actual number available to the U.S. aboard their carriers and based on Midway Island itself provided them with a small margin of 23 aircraft more than the 325 aboard the Japanese carriers. However, the numbers game counted for little in these circumstances, as every U.S. type employed in the battle was inferior to its Japanese counterpart to a greater or lesser degree.

While the main Navy fighter, the F4F-4 Wildcat, was inferior to the "Zero," U.S. pilots had learned through bitter experience the tactics necessary to take on their more maneuverable opponent. Whenever possible, the F4F-4s would dive on the "Zeros," using the fire from their six machine guns to destroy

the lightly loaded and unarmored airframe of the Japanese fighter. Where dogfighting could not be avoided, the Wildcat had shown itself able to take on the "Zero." U.S. Navy pilots were highly trained in deflection shooting, and their reflector gunsights offered accurate gunnery which allowed a high probability of lethal hits. The presence of armor and self-sealing fuel tanks also enabled the portly Wildcat to take the sort of damage that would destroy a "Zero-Sen" and still return to its carrier. The F4F was the mount of Lt. Commander John S. "Jimmy" Thach, who at Midway commanded the composite fighter squadron composed of the *Saratoga*'s VF-3 and *Yorktown*'s VF-5. His experience fighting the "Zero-Sen" had led to his formulation of a new tactic that took his name, the "Thach Weave," which he and VF-3 employed with success in the battle of Midway.

Although the Douglas SBD Dauntless was regarded by the Navy as obsolete by the time of Midway, it was in all probability one of the best dive bombers in the world at the time. Its virtue lay in its great stability and light control responses. At Midway it was to prove to be the real killer of the Japanese carriers when, at the end of its rock-steady dive at an optimum angle of 80 degrees, it was to deposit its 1,000lb bombs deep in the vitals of the enemy vessels. It was, however, the torpedo bomber pilots who flew the most decidedly obsolescent of the major U.S. Navy types employed in the Midway battle. The TBD-1 Devastator had been designed as far back as 1934. In 1937, when it first entered service with the Navy, it was the best of its type in the world, but by 1942 it was totally outmoded. At the time of Midway, however, it was the only torpedo bomber the Navy possessed in any numbers because its replacement, the Grumman TBF-1, was not yet available in sufficient quantities. Indeed, the 21 crews from *Hornet*'s Torpedo Bombing Squadron Eight (VT-8), who had been converting to the new airplane in the United States, arrived at Pearl one day after the *Hornet* had departed for Midway. Not only were the torpedo bombing crews thus condemned to fly against the Japanese carriers in an airplane that was laboriously slow and had a poor rate of climb, but they were also forearmed with the knowledge that its poor performance in its designated role was compounded by the ignominious reputation of its nominated main weapon, the unreliable Mk.13 torpedo. Its record at Midway was one of glorious failure for, as we shall see, it was the sacrifice of the TBD crews that opened the roof for the dive-bombers to destroy the Japanese carriers.

Whereas the Navy at least was flying some modern types, Marine Corps Air Group 22 (MAG 22) on Midway itself was operating decidedly obsolete navy "hand-me-downs" in the form of Brewster F2A-3 Buffalo fighters, nicknamed "Flying Coffins," and Vought SB2U-3 Vindicator dive-bombers. The latter were disparagingly nicknamed "vibrators" by their pilots, and had the disconcerting habit of shedding their wing fabric, which was repaired by the liberal application of sticky tape. Some new equipment was available in the form of seven F4F-3s serving alongside the Buffaloes of VMF-221 and some sixteen SBDs operating with the Vindicators of VMSB-241. In the case of the latter, their potential effectiveness was offset by the Marine pilots' virtual lack of flying experience on the type.

To beef up Marine air power on the island, both the Army and the Navy dispatched a hotchpotch of types. The Army sent a detachment of its 7th Army Air Force, made up of nineteen B-17 Flying Fortresses and four of the new B-26 Marauder medium bombers, equipped to carry single torpedoes under their fuselages. Much was expected of the for-

mer type, but its contribution to the battle was negligible, in spite of the great amount of space it took up on the small Eastern Island air base and the prodigious quantities of fuel used in the B-17 sorties. Offensive navy air assets on the island were confined to six of the TBFs from VT-8 that had arrived at Pearl on 29 May. From among the crews that had disembarked with the new airplanes, six were selected to fly out to Midway, arriving on 1 June.

Most important of all the aircraft types based on Midway were the Navy PBY-5 and -5A Catalina amphibious flying boats of Patrol Wings 1 and 2. They had the vital role of searching out and reporting on the advancing Japanese forces, and by 30 May no fewer than two dozen PBYs were sweeping a huge arc from the NNE to the SSW of Midway out to a distance of 700 miles. Day in and day out the PBYs would lift their overladen airframes into the air to begin the long haul out to the maximum point of their ocean sweep. However, it was only on 3 June, the date identified by Hypo as the earliest feasible for the start of the Japanese offensive, that the imminence of a Japanese invasion of Midway was finally revealed to the aircrews. With the search pattern of the PBYs now covering all likely approaches to Midway, it was only a matter of time before the rapidly closing Japanese forces were seen and the curtain arose on one of the most decisive battles in the history of warfare.

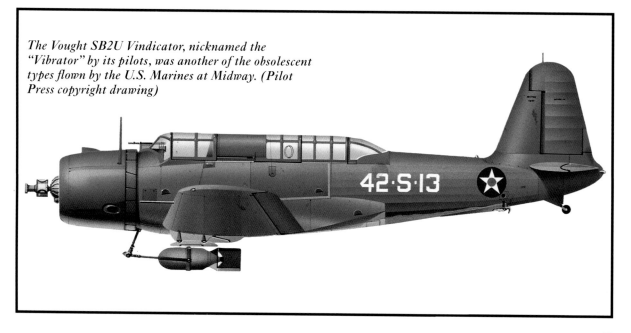

*The Vought SB2U Vindicator, nicknamed the "Vibrator" by its pilots, was another of the obsolescent types flown by the U.S. Marines at Midway. (Pilot Press copyright drawing)*

# THE BATTLE: 3 JUNE

## Combat Is Joined

The first act in the great drama now unfolding opened many hundreds of miles from Midway island when, shortly after 0300, the carriers *Ryujo* and *Junyo* launched their aircraft to attack Dutch Harbor and thus initiate the combat phase of Operation AL. However, owing to the prevalence of the fog and generally bad weather so characteristic of the region, *Junyo*'s attack force of fifteen "Val" dive-bombers and thirteen escorting "Zeros" was unable to locate the target and returned to the carrier. *Ryujo*'s air group had better luck, and nine of her "Kate" bombers and three of her "Zeros" found a break in the cloud which revealed their target directly below them at about 0808. Radar aboard a seaplane tender in the harbor detected the incoming Japanese strike group, and, although the vessels in the harbor could not make their escape, the antiaircraft defenses were forewarned and were able to put up a heavy barrage. The "Zeros" also tangled with a number of P-40s that managed to get aloft.

Although damage was inflicted on the base, another raid scheduled for 0945, to attack the naval vessels in the harbor, was launched. The inclement weather hid the target, forcing the aircraft to return to their carriers, but not before they had tangled with some U.S. fighters in the process, losing a "Zero" fighter. At midday, with the aircraft recov-

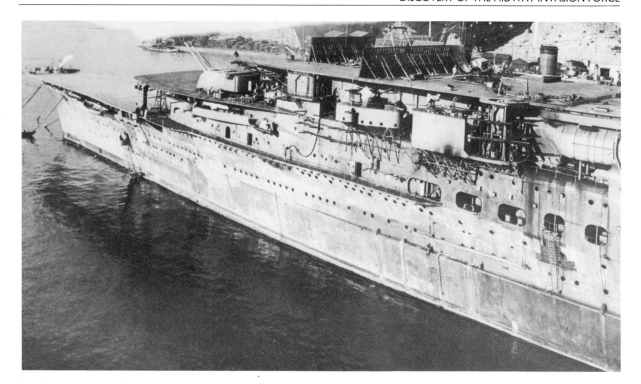

ered, Admiral, Kakuta turned his force to the southwest.

Two days later another strike was made on Dutch Harbor which completed the destruction of the oil farm and further damaged other installations. The Army Air Force responded by launching raids by B-17s and B-26s, but they achieved no hits on the Japanese vessels. By the time his airplanes were landing, Kakuta had been told by Yamamoto that, because of events in the Midway battle, Operation AL was suspended and he and his carriers were to stand by for action to the south. Although the invasion of Adak was canceled, Attu and Kiska were occupied on 5 and 7 June as planned. Nevertheless, the whole AL operation was a pointless exercise, failing totally in its aim. Admiral Nimitz was never in doubt that the attack on the Aleutians

*▲ Completed three years after her consort, the* **Kaga** *("Increased Joy") shared the common origin as a battle cruiser and was likewise completed with three flight decks forward. In this form she had a maximum capacity of 60 aircraft. (via Roger Chesneau)*

was anything more than a diversionary sideshow, and in terms of the wider battle about to begin that is what it remained. Some hours after the first attack on Dutch Harbor, sightings by PBYs on air patrol far to the southeast of Midway Island were to herald the start of the main battle.

### Discovery of the Midway Invasion Force

The first contact with the approaching Japanese forces was made by PBY number 6-V-55, whose pilot, Ensign Charles Eaton, reported the sighting of two cargo vessels at 0904. But it was the broadcast some 21 minutes later from another PBY flown by Ensign "Jack" Reid that electrified the Midway garrison. At the extreme limit of their PBY's patrol search, the crew of 8-V-55 had spotted a group of ships on the horizon. This prompted Reid to dispatch the message "Sighted Main Body," followed a few minutes later by "Bearing 262, distance 700 miles." Demanding greater clarification of the

*◄ The Kawanishi H8K "Emily" was the most powerful and formidable long-range flying boat used by any of the combatants in the Second World War. Planned reconnaissances of Pearl Harbor by two of these aircraft between 31 May and 3 June, to provide up-* *to-date intelligence of U.S. fleet movements before the attack on Midway, had to be abandoned. Additionally, failure of the submarine cordon to do the same left Nagumo totally devoid of any real knowledge of the U.S. fleet's whereabouts. (Philip Jarrett)*

41

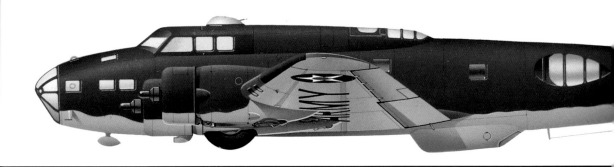

*Although a number of raids on elements of the Japanese Fleet were launched by U.S. Army B-17s on Midway, no hits were registered on any warships. (Pilot Press copyright drawing)*

sightings, for they were not prepared to release their air assets on the strength of such vague reports, Shannon and Simmard then had to wait some hours before they received from the PBY pilot the detailed information they desired.

Hampered by clear skies devoid of any protective cloud cover, Ensign Reid had to change course and altitude frequently to avoid detection and secure the most efficacious position whereby he could obtain accurate information on the makeup of the Japanese force. Approaching from astern, he saw laid out before him Rear Admiral Tanaka's

Midway Invasion Force, cruising at a stately 19kts with the light cruiser *Jintsu* steaming between and at the head of two parallel columns of transport vessels. To their fore in an arc plowed the ten screening destroyers. The report he now filed was received on Midway at 1125, and in it Reid counted eleven vessels, identifying them as a small carrier, one seaplane carrier, two battleships, several cruisers and several destroyers. The variety of warship

▼ **Kaga** *underwent major reconstruction between 1934 and 1935 which saw her displacement raised from 26,900 tons to 38,200 tons. Her triple deck was replaced by a single much lengthened flight deck and* *her aviation component increased to 90 aircraft. She and* **Akagi** *formed the First Carrier Division of the Rengo Kantai. (via Roger Chesneau)*

▶ *This shows the approach of the Japanese forces of Operation MI toward Midway up until 0900 of 3 June, when Tanaka's invasion force was spotted by PBY 8-V-55, flown by Ensign "Jack" Reid. By that time Task Force 16 (A) had been joined by Fletcher's Task Force 17* *(B) at Point Luck (PL). Both Task Forces had avoided the Japanese submarine cordon put in place by Yamamoto specifically for the purpose of detecting their departure from Pearl Harbor.*

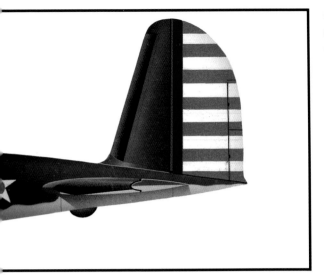

only saw Tanaka's Invasion Force, but also flew across the track of Kondo's "Main Body," Kurita's Close Support Force and Fujita's Seaplane Tender Group, all of which were operating in close proximity to one another. Despite Reid's inaccurate identification of some of the vessels in Tanaka's convoy, it was clear that a sizable Japanese force was now heading on a direct course for Midway. This knowledge allowed Simmard to give the green light to release the Army pilots for an air strike.

As Reid's PBY turned for home and disappeared over the horizon, a message from *Jintsu* had already flashed through the air, breaking the blanket Japanese radio silence and conveying the news to the flagship that the Invasion Force had been discovered by American aircraft 600 miles from Midway. Up to this point all was seen to be going well, and accounts indicate that the Commander in Chief and his staff aboard *Yamato* were all in fine fettle. Tanaka's broadcast, however, put an immediate dampener on proceedings with the realization

types suggests that Reid's report was, unbeknown to himself, based upon a composite sighting. In all probability this resulted from his frequent maneuvering in the intervening hours since his initial message to Midway, in the process of which he not

# The Fleets Converge

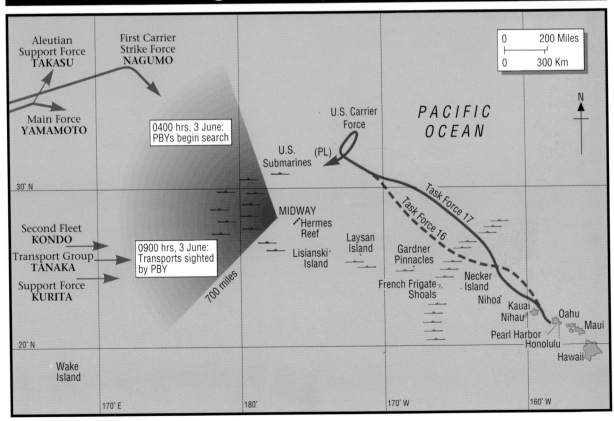

▲ *The carrier* Soryu *("Green Dragon"), seen here under construction at the Kure Naval Yard, was built under the limitations of the* *Washington Treaty. She was formally commissioned into the Combined Fleet on 29 December 1937. (via Roger Chesneau)*

▼ *Although quite small and cramped internally because of the limitations treaty, the* Soryu *still carried a respectable 63 aircraft. She formed the* *other half of Carrier Division 2 of the Rengo Kantai.*

that the enemy had established contact with the advancing fleet much earlier than the operational plan had allowed for. As matters now stood, the Commander in Chief and his staff could only reconcile themselves to the premature initiation of combat and the inevitability of early air attacks on Tanaka's Invasion Force.

Of the aircraft on Midway, only the Army B-17s had the range to mount an effective attack on the Japanese force at this distance. Even so, it had been necessary to fit an extra fuel tank in each of their bomb bays, reducing the actual offensive load carried by half, to just four 500lb bombs apiece. Shortly after 1225 nine Flying Fortresses under the command of Lt. Colonel Walter Sweeney took off, heading westward in the general direction of Reid's last sighting fix. It was 1640 before they located the Japanese force and began their high-level bombing runs. Far below, *Jintsu* and her ten screening destroyers opened up at the rapidly moving shapes above them with their antiaircraft batteries, but the effectiveness of their fire was more apparent than real, for none of the B-17s was hit. In turn, the American bombers failed to hit any of the Japanese ships, although the great waterspouts raised close

to a number of the vessels prompted some totally unjustified claims by the pilots on return to Midway. In their debriefings, pilots and crews spoke of hits on six vessels including two transports, two heavy cruisers and even two battleships. On the presumption that these vessels were now flame-wracked hulks, the submarine USS *Cuttlefish*, which was patrolling in the vicinity, was sent to sink them. Not surprisingly, it was unable to find any trace of the purported wrecks.

Very early the following morning Tanaka's as yet unscathed force was subjected to another, smaller but more successful air attack. Four of the lumbering and vulnerable PBYs had been jury-rigged to carry single torpedoes, and with volunteer crews had taken off from Midway at 2115 late on 4 June with the intention of attacking the Japanese force. Three

▼ *Fitting out at the Yokosuka Naval Yard, next to either the Combined Fleet flagship* **Nagato** *or her sister ship* **Mutsu**, *is the* **Hiryu***. She was the last carrier built by the Japanese under the* *restrictions of the Washington Naval Treaty. Commissioned into the Fleet on 5 July 1939 she shared with* **Akagi** *the unusual distinction of carrying her island on the port side.*

reached the convoy, fixing its position with their onboard radar, and, by taking advantage of the bright moonlight which silhouetted the enemy vessels, began their attack at 0130. Only the PBY flown by Ensign Probst registered a hit, his torpedo detonating close to the bow of the oiler *Akebono Maru*. The explosion killed eleven of her crew and wounded a further thirteen, but the damage to the vessel was successfully contained and she was soon able to reposition herself in the convoy. The PBYs succeeded in escaping the hail of antiaircraft fire sent aloft by the Japanese vessels, and proceeded in their slow plodding fashion to head back to Mid-

way. They arrived back just as the air attack by Nagumo's strike force was beginning.

### Task Forces 16 and 17

The tone on board the *Enterprise* and *Hornet* had been set the previous day, when Spruance signaled to the vessels of his Task Force the essence of the plan formulated to deal with the expected Japanese carrier force heading for Midway. A remarkably dispassionate affair, it nevertheless conveyed in its matter-of-factness a subdued confidence. Somewhat later on the same day the planned and vital rendezvous at Point Luck took place, with Fletcher officially taking over tactical command of both carrier groups, although in practice the two Task Forces were to operate independently. Radio silence was absolute, even the use of the intership communication system, which was believed secure from

▼ Enterprise – *the Big "E" – is regarded by many as the greatest warship to serve with the U.S. Navy. Launched on 3 October* 1936, *she served gallantly throughout the conflict only to be unceremoniously scrapped afterward. (via Roger Chesneau)*

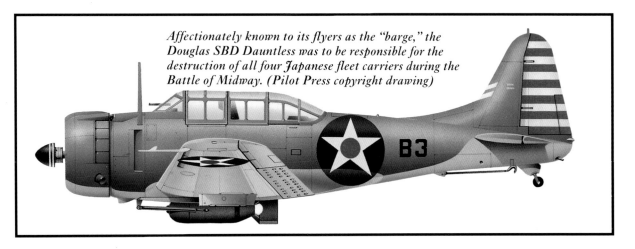

*Affectionately known to its flyers as the "barge," the Douglas SBD Dauntless was to be responsible for the destruction of all four Japanese fleet carriers during the Battle of Midway. (Pilot Press copyright drawing)*

signal leakage, being suspended. 3 June saw the three carriers and their escorts plowing a zigzag course in and around the vicinity of Point Luck, with Fletcher and Spruance patiently waiting for Nagumo's carriers to show their hand.

The day had not been without its drama, however. Both Nimitz and Fletcher had been party to the news of Ensign Reid's discovery of Tanaka's Invasion Force in the early morning, and the possibility had always existed that his description of the enemy force as the "Main Body" would be accepted by one or either of them as just that. Nimitz, however, saw nothing, even in the more detailed reports received later in the morning regarding the makeup of the enemy force, to make him doubt the intelligence advice given to him by Hypo that the main Japanese striking force lay in Nagumo's carriers, and that they had yet to make their appearance. Fletcher had also reached this conclusion, receiving confirmation from Nimitz late that afternoon in a coded message flashed to the *Yorktown*: "That is not repeat not the enemy striking force – stop – That is the landing force. The striking force will hit from the northwest at daylight tomorrow." With the clock now beginning to run ever faster, Fletcher ordered that *Enterprise* and *Hornet* be flashed a course change, and at 1950 the two Task Forces headed south through the night, aiming for a point approximately 200 miles north of Midway. Assuming that Nagumo would turn up as predicted by intelligence, it was from here that Fletcher intended to launch his airplanes against the Japanese carriers early on the following day.

### First Air Fleet

3 June was a day of frantic preparations aboard the four carriers of the First Air Fleet. Final refueling had been completed, and shortly after 0600 the five

▲ *Regarded as the half-sister of the* Soryu, *the* Hiryu *("Flying Dragon") was the flagship of Carrier Division 2 and carried the pennant of Vice Admiral Tamon Yamaguchi at Pearl Harbor through to her destruction at Midway.* Hiryu *was the only Japanese carrier to launch a successful strike on the U.S. carriers during the battle. (via Roger Chesneau)*

oilers of the supply train and their escorting destroyer, the *Akigumo*, fell away. The carriers and their escorts then turned to the southeast and accelerated to 24kts to begin the final run in toward Midway. Deep in the bowels of the carriers, mechanics labored long and hard on the engines of the aircraft to ensure optimum performance, while the armorers loaded belts of bullets and shells into the machine guns and cannon. Others made ready the bombs and their shackles in preparation for the attack scheduled for the early hours of the following morning. From the bridge of the flagship, Admiral Nagumo observed the scene about him. A tight defensive ring had been formed around the four carriers by the fast battleships *Haruna* and *Kirishima*, along with the heavy cruisers *Tone* and *Chikuma*, the light cruiser *Nagara* and the 12 destroyers of the screening force. Symptomatic, perhaps, of the rise in tension was a false sighting of enemy aircraft in the early evening by the watch on the *Tone*, and although three "Zeros" were launched from the *Akagi* to investigate, nothing was found.

Down below, the pilots detailed for the Midway strike relaxed or slept as the mood took them, while others, perhaps more mindful of their own mortality, took time to visit one of the small Shinto shrines on board, invoking the protection of its *kami* in the trial to come. All through the fleet there was the growing awareness that in a matter of hours the enemy would be engaged, in the greatest battle ever fought by the Combined Fleet. From the lowliest sailor to the most senior officer there exuded the almost tangible expectation of certain victory in the hours and days ahead.

▼ *The dive-bombing squadrons of the First Carrier Striking Force at Midway were equipped with the Aichi D3A1 dive-bomber. Code-named "Val" by the Allies, the type had notched up many successes since the start of the Pacific War.*

# THE BATTLE: 4 JUNE

## First Air Fleet Strikes Midway

In the hours before 0245, at which time the aircrew were awoken aboard *Akagi*, *Kaga*, *Hiryu* and *Soryu*, until 0430, when the first aircraft of the Midway attack group were launched, the carriers of the First Air Fleet were hives of intense activity. The regular and persistent metallic clang and associated hum of hydraulic lines reverberated through the carriers as lifts raised the fully fueled and armed airplanes of the first strike wave from the hangar levels below to the flight deck. The whole process of physically manhandling and spotting aircraft in their correct positions on the flight deck was tiring but exacting work. First came the large "Kate" level bombers, which were positioned at the rear of the flight line, followed in their turn by the dive-bombers. The last to be placed were the "Zero-Sen" fighters, which would be the first to launch, providing the protective umbrella below which their heavier brethren would seek safety. At 0300 engines spluttered then roared into life as mechanics began to warm them up. Below decks, pilots of the first strike wave donned flying suits before moving through the narrow passageways to the galleys, where breakfast preceded a final briefing. Many were in a state of nervous but excited anticipation, as this was their first combat mission. The employment of the younger replacement pilots in the first attack wave was a deliberate ploy by Nagumo. He was retaining the majority of his veteran flyers aboard the carriers to form a second strike force, and thus ensure against the possibility of American carriers making an appearance.

While this was symptomatic of his natural caution, even Nagumo had no real reason at this stage to suppose that such an eventuality was likely. he perceived the intelligence picture as altogether quite rosy. Having been denied any knowledge of the premature discovery of Tanaka's invasion force on the previous day by Yamamoto's continuing insistence on radio silence, he had no reason to believe that the anticipated element of surprise, deemed so important for this stage of the operation, would not be achieved. Such optimism is implicit in the intelligence appraisal that he circulated to senior commanders shortly before operations commenced:

1. The enemy fleet will probably come to engage

▶ *No photograph survives from Japanese sources showing the air operations of the Nagumo Fleet at Midway. Although this picture dates from just prior to the Pearl Harbor strike in December 1941, nevertheless it conveys very well a scene similar to that experienced aboard the flagship* Akagi *as it prepared to launch its "Zero" fighters early on the morning of 4 June 1942.*

when the Midway landing operations are begun.

2. Enemy air patrols from Midway will be heavier to westward and southward, less heavy to the north and northwest.

3. The radius of enemy air patrols is estimated to be approximately 500 miles.

4. The enemy is not yet aware of our plan, and he has not yet detected our task force.

5. There is no evidence of an enemy task force in our vicinity.

6. It is possible for us to attack Midway, destroy the land-based planes there, and support landing operations. We can then turn around, meet an approaching enemy task force, and destroy it.

7. Possible counterattacks by enemy land-based aircraft can surely be repulsed by our interceptors and antiaircraft fire.

Apart from point 7, which was shortly to receive dramatic verification, the other observations were hopelessly in error. Such self-deception goes far to explain the tardiness with which the Japanese now approached the whole matter of aerial reconnaissance, on which the security of the carrier force turned.

Mitsuo Fuchida, the designated first strike leader until illness rendered him *hors de combat* shortly after leaving Japan, observed that provision for reconnaissance was made on the basis of a single-phase search, the airplanes being despatched only after the launch of the Midway strike force. Assuming that all went according to plan, any American force within the search arc would be located and dealt with by Nagumo's second strike wave. While believing the single-phase search plan adequate (see Map 3), he harbored doubts concerning its efficacy as a result of difficulties experienced

in its employment during the Indian Ocean operation, when enemy surface vessels had been spotted only after air groups from the carriers were already attacking other targets. The limitation of the single-phase search was that it was sufficient only to confirm, as he somewhat pithily observed, what the Japanese already believed – that there was no American force in the area. This failure to instigate a more thorough search procedure, which would of necessity have required the employment of far more aircraft than the few allotted, also stemmed from a great reluctance to employ combat aircraft such as the "Kate" and "Val," which possessed the necessary range for such tasks, at the expense of strapping a bomb or torpedo underneath them and using them for offensive purposes. There can be no doubting the impact of inadequate reconnaissance methods on Japanese fortunes in the battle about to commence. Minoru Genda, Air Officer of the Air Fleet, reflecting after the battle, admitted that the search plan was negligent and that in consequence it proved to be "the initial cause for the Midway defeat."

Having received their final briefing, the aircrew on the four carriers emerged on to their respective

▶ *It was Minoru Genda, Air Officer of the First Air Fleet and serving with Nagumo's staff on board* **Akagi,** *who was to observe that the slipshod nature of the air search plan illustrated here was the initial cause of the Japanese defeat at Midway. Notwithstanding the*

*failure to instigate a much more comprehensive plan, using more aircraft, the delay in launching* **Tone** *and* **Chikuma's** *floatplanes was to deny Nagumo the earlier sighting of Task Force 16 and 17 that would have resulted, had they been launched when originally intended, at 0430.*

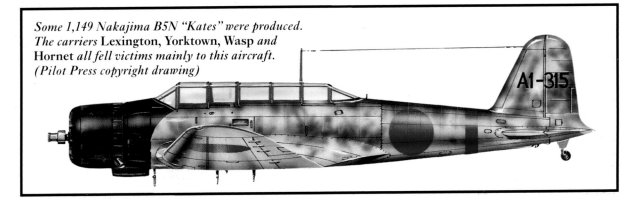

*Some 1,149 Nakajima B5N "Kates" were produced. The carriers* **Lexington, Yorktown, Wasp** *and* **Hornet** *all fell victims mainly to this aircraft. (Pilot Press copyright drawing)*

# Air Search Patterns of First Carrier Air Fleet, 0430 onward, 4 June

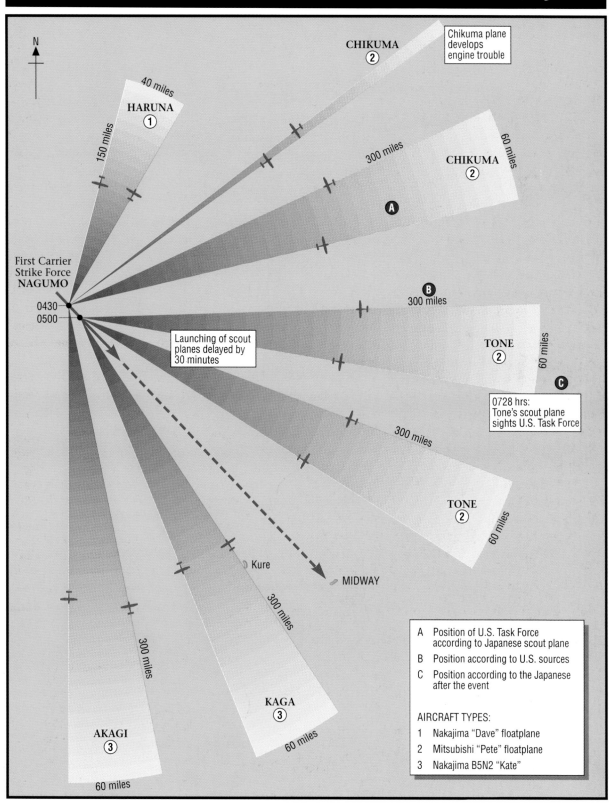

N

Chikuma plane develops engine trouble

CHIKUMA
②

40 miles

HARUNA
①

150 miles

300 miles

CHIKUMA
②

60 miles

A

First Carrier
Strike Force
NAGUMO

0430
0500

Launching of scout
planes delayed by
30 minutes

B
300 miles

TONE
②

60 miles

C

0728 hrs:
Tone's scout plane
sights U.S. Task Force

300 miles

TONE
②

60 miles

Kure

300 miles

MIDWAY

300 miles

A    Position of U.S. Task Force
     according to Japanese scout plane
B    Position according to U.S. sources
C    Position according to the Japanese
     after the event

AIRCRAFT TYPES:
1    Nakajima "Dave" floatplane
2    Mitsubishi "Pete" floatplane
3    Nakajima B5N2 "Kate"

KAGA
③

AKAGI
③

60 miles

60 miles

decks and proceeded to board their aircraft. Engines were turned over and sprang into life as the 108 aircraft of the first wave warmed up for takeoff. With their flight decks illuminated by floodlights, all four carriers turned into the wind. From their respective bridges green lights flashed on, and, as the roar of the engines rose to a crescendo, the first of 36 "Zero" fighters, led by Lieutenant Masuharu Suginami from the *Soryu*, launched promptly at 0430. Against a backdrop of cheering deckhands and waving white caps 36 "Val" dive-bombers launched from *Akagi* and *Kaga*, with 36 "Kate" level bombers from *Soryu* and *Hiryu*, under the respective commands of Lt. Shoichi Ogawa and raid leader Lt. Joicho Tomonaga. One by one the aircraft took up station amid the huge formation circling the fleet. Fifteen minutes after launching had started, Tomonaga gave the order and all 108 aircraft of the First Strike Wave turned to the southeast and headed toward Midway.

No sooner had they departed than the lifts on the carriers were delivering more aircraft onto the decks. Just nine "Zeros" were sent aloft from *Kaga* to provide a combat air patrol for the 21 vessels of the fleet, with another nine spotted on *Akagi*'s flight deck as a contingency reserve. This was hardly a sufficient strength to suggest expectation of enemy attack, and was no doubt symptomatic of the general air of confidence pervading the fleet.

The next air elements launched comprised the reconnaissance types, all of which were due to take off promptly at 0430. *Haruna*'s floatplane catapulted as planned. *Kaga* and *Akagi* launched their D3A1s to begin their air searches to the south and

▲ *The main benefit to the Americans of the Japanese attack on the Aleutians was their recovery of an almost intact example of an A6M2 "Zero" flown by Flight Petty Officer Tadayoshi Koga of the* **Ryujo.** *He had been killed attempting to land the slightly damaged airplane on the tundra. By repairing the aircraft the Americans were able to determine its strong and weak points, helping them to develop tactics to combat it as well as influencing the design of the Wildcat's replacement, the Grumman F6 Hellcat.*

southeast of Midway itself. However, the two Mitsubishi "Pete" floatplanes of the heavy cruiser *Chikuma* did not get aloft until five and eight minutes past the due launch time. Even more unfortunate for the Japanese was the delay on her sister ship, *Tone*. While one of her floatplanes was catapulted off at 0442, the second was not finally sent aloft until 0500, some 30min after the planned launch time. Whatever the subsequent explanations offered for these delays, and they ranged from troublesome engines and catapults to simple sloppiness of procedure, the consequences of those lost minutes were very shortly to prove fatal to the fortunes of the First Air Fleet.

### Midway Island: 0300–0700

Following reveille at 0300, Midway rapidly became a scene of purposeful activity as the many aircraft squeezed onto the small island base were prepared for the decisive events of the coming day. Half an hour before the Japanese strike wave took off from their carriers, eleven of the amphibious PBYs lumbered down the runway, hauling their overloaded and inelegant airframes into the air and out over the wide expanse of the Pacific to begin the search that would surely provide, before the morning was much older, the first sightings of Nagumo's carriers. Shortly thereafter, against the backdrop of dawn's early light, Lt. Colonel Sweeney's force of 16 Army B-17s was once more sent aloft to visit further destruction on Tanaka's invasion force, still plowing its slow course toward Midway. With the "big boys" now departed, the rest of the aircraft spread across the base were armed with bombs and torpedoes and made ready for action. Engines were started and given their preliminary warm-up, their pulsating throb reverberating through the cool of the early morning air.

On both islands of the atoll base, Marines called to their weapons checked their ammunition and practiced last-minute gunnery drill, elevating and rotating their pieces while tensely awaiting the first radar sighting of the incoming enemy. Although the two sets on the base were somewhat dated, their maximum detection range of 150 miles gave valuable early warning time. There would be no catching aircraft on the ground this time, as at Pearl Harbor.

Events now began to move quickly. Between 0520 and 0553 a series of sightings from PBYs and on the ground radar galvanized the whole base into frenetic activity. The initial sighting was relayed by a PBY of Flight 58, commanded by Lieutenant Howard P. Ady, at 0520. He reported spotting a Japanese reconnaissance airplane. At 0530 came the words that those on Midway, in Fletcher's Task Force and on Oahu, had been waiting so tensely to

hear: "Carrier bearing 320, distance 180." The order now went out to the pilots to man their aircraft. By 0545 all were ready, with engines turning over, awaiting the word to launch. Some minutes later a further flash was received from a second PBY, flying a pattern adjacent to that of Flight 58. It stated that many airplanes were heading toward Midway on a bearing of 320 degrees. This provided both Midway and Fletcher with the absolutely vital information that Nagumo had committed his first strike wave, and that it was inbound to the atoll base.

In the meantime, life had become decidedly more hazardous for the shadowing PBYs. Far below, keen eyes on the Japanese vessels had spotted one of the Catalinas drifting across the sky, and heavy anti-aircraft fire had opened up on the unwelcome observers, littering the sky around them with ugly smudges of black smoke. "Zero" fighters had launched from *Kaga* in a bid to shoot down the intruders, but by making good use of the cloud cover the two PBYs successfully avoided them. Finally, at 0552 Lieutenant Ady was able to despatch the clinching sighting fix on Nagumo's force, reporting: "Two carriers and battleships bearing 320 degrees, distance 180 course 135, speed 25." Barely a minute thereafter Midway obtained its own radar sighting, when operators poring over their scopes in the shack on Sand Island detected the incoming Japanese strike force at a range of 93 miles and an altitude of 11,000ft. As they moved ever closer to Midway the blips rapidly resolved into one large formation, denoting the approach of a sizable enemy force. Without further ado the order was given to send off the aircraft.

▶ *The pilot of a D3A1 "Val" carrying a single 1,050lb bomb under its centerline opens its throttle as it gains speed for takeoff. The "Vals" in the Midway strike came from* **Kaga** *and* **Akagi***.*

*Woefully obsolescent by the time of Midway, the Douglas TBD Devastators from the three U.S. carriers were decimated in their attacks on Nagumo's fleet. (Pilot Press copyright drawing)*

As the air raid siren wailed over Midway the Wildcat and Buffalo fighters of VMF-221 took off and, once aloft, headed for the Japanese formation. In their wake the pilots of the bombing aircraft taxied their charges to the runway and prepared in rapid succession to take off before the arrival of the enemy. The first aloft were the dive-bombers of VMSB-241 – sixteen Marine TBDs led by Major Lofton Henderson, each armed with a 500lb bomb, followed by the venerable SB2U "Vibrators" under the command of Major Benjamin Norris. Thereafter came the six Navy TBFs of VT-6 and the four Army B-26 medium bombers, these two new types making their combat debut. By 0620, with the enemy force just 22 miles from Midway, the airbase on Eastern Island lay deserted, and its former occupants were heading at their best speed toward the northwest and the position of the last sighting of the Japanese carriers, in response to the simple but graphic order ". . . attack enemy carriers." Set to join this motley collection of types was Sweeney's force of Flying Fortresses, which was already far out to sea when it received new orders at 0600 to divert and head for the more significant target of Nagumo's carriers. The somewhat limited chances of survival of this uncoordinated, ill-experienced and poorly equipped force had been further reduced by the decision not to employ the Wildcats and Buffaloes as fighter cover for the bombers. Instead, contrary to Nimitz's original orders, they were to be used to protect the airfield.

At 0616 the 25 Buffaloes and Wildcats under the command of Majors Parks and Armistead acquired their first clear picture of Tomonaga's approaching force. Climbing before the advancing Japanese, Parks was able to secure a height advantage, and with his section of twelve fighters began his diving attack on the level bombers, with Armistead's group in tow. The "Zeros," flying top cover, were stationed slightly behind the formation of level- and dive-bombers, and although they were not initially well placed to respond to the attackers, they were able to use their superior speed and maneuverability to place themselves rapidly on the tails of the slower American fighters.

Within a few minutes a wild and confused swirling mêlée filled the sky, and it quickly became apparent that the Japanese fighters had the upper hand. The "Zeros" assailed the Buffaloes and Wildcats with their machine guns and cannon, hacking them from the air. Nevertheless, the gallant impression made by the Marine pilots was enough for one of *Soryu's* pilots to misidentify the portly and obsolescent Buffaloes and report that they had been attacked by "30 to 40 F4F-3s at a point some 20 miles from Midway." The Japanese tally for this few minutes of vicious dogfighting was thirteen Buffaloes and two Wildcats shot down, with Major Parks among the pilots lost. Nagumo was later to record that three level-bombers and two "Zeros" were shot down by the Marine pilots while inbound to Midway.

Emerging from the attack virtually unscathed, Tomonaga led the formation on the final run-in to

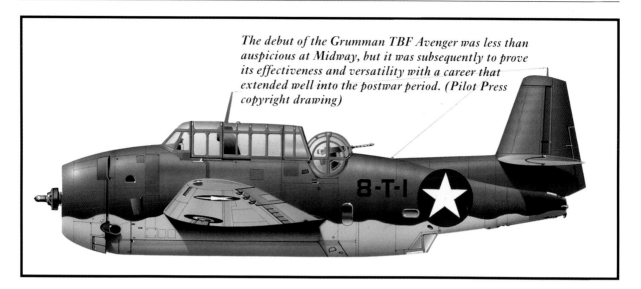

*The debut of the Grumman TBF Avenger was less than auspicious at Midway, but it was subsequently to prove its effectiveness and versatility with a career that extended well into the postwar period. (Pilot Press copyright drawing)*

Midway, although it was frustratingly obvious that the airbase was devoid of airplanes. The bulk of the level-bombers therefore directed their attention on Sand Island, hits on the oil tanks starting fires that lasted for days. In their wake, Chihaya's dive-bombers plummeted down, targeting the hangars and other installations with their 500lb bombs while the "Zeros," now released from their defensive tasks, swooped in at low level, strafing ground targets. The defending fire was of such an order that it was later described by the attackers as "vicious." Official Japanese sources admitted the loss of four aircraft over Midway itself. The captain of the Japanese submarine *I-168*, which was lying offshore ten miles to the south of Midway, had an excellent view of the raid, and later spoke of the island being turned into a mass of flames with buildings and fuel tanks exploding.

Nevertheless, when Tomonaga gave the order for the raiding force to withdraw at 0643 it was clear to his experienced eye that, in many respects, the raid had not succeeded. U.S. air power on the island had not been neutralized, and would still be able to use the runways which, most surprisingly, remained undamaged. Neither had the bombing eliminated the bulk of the heavy weapons on the island, and these would certainly be used to oppose the landing of the invasion force. Tomonaga was some minutes into the return flight before he decided what he thought needed to be done. At 0700 he had a message flashed to Nagumo: "There is need of a second attack wave." Within moments of receiving his raid

leader's signal, Nagumo himself had just reason for believing Tomonaga's request to be sound.

### Task Forces 16 and 17: 0430–0838

Even as Lt. Suginami opened the throttle of his "Zero" and accelerated down the flight deck of the *Soryu* on the dot of 0430, some 220 miles away to the east ten TBDs from the USS *Yorktown* were ordered aloft by Admiral Fletcher to scout the arc of sea 100 miles to the north of Task Forces 16 and 17. Although he was convinced that intelligence was correct in believing Nagumo would strike at Midway from the northwest, in the absence of any firm information he had no intention of allowing the Japanese admiral to catch him with his pants down should he decide to approach the island via a more northerly track. With the last of the scout airplanes dispatched, the orderly waiting routine of the past few days was reestablished, although it was clear that tension was slowly beginning to build as the minutes ticked away.

Aboard *Yorktown* and *Enterprise* Fletcher and Spruance sat patiently waiting for news of the first sighting of the Japanese force. When it came, Lt. Ady's initial message contained nothing on which the Task Force commanders could act. However, the message received on *Enterprise* at 0534 not only gave news of the sighting of a carrier, but also contained a vital direction fix on which Spruance could plan his reaction. In principle it had already been determined. Fletcher and Spruance were in agreement that only an all-out strike on the Japanese carriers, launched at the earliest possible moment, would suffice to yield maximum advantage. This explains Spruance's order to his chief of staff that *Enterprise* and *Hornet* be ready to launch everything they had at the earliest possible moment. However, the receipt of later messages sighting Nagumo's inbound Midway strike force, allied to a second fix on two carriers, placed the Japanese force about 200 miles from the American position and prompted the admiral to make a rapid reappraisal of the situation.

Spruance had originally intended to close to half that distance before launching his air strike, but it now became clear that by doing so he would forego the opportunity to realize his principal aim of inflicting maximum damage on the Japanese carriers. He estimated that Tomonaga's strike group would recover aboard their respective carriers at about 0900 and would then be rearmed for a second strike. They would then be at their most vulnerable to an American air attack. To catch them Spruance would have to launch very soon, at least two hours earlier than originally intended, even though to reach Nagumo's carriers at that distance involved a round trip that lay beyond the maximum range of his torpedo bombers. It was presumed that Nagumo would have to maintain his present heading to recover his aircraft, and an intercept course was plotted whereby he could be brought within the maximum strike range of 200 miles by about 0700.

Fletcher also had reason to reflect on the implications of the sightings, governed as he was by his experiences in the Coral Sea. As only two Japanese carriers had been spotted, he decided to hold *Yorktown*'s air group in reserve, pending the receipt of more accurate information locating the other two, or possibly three carriers which intelligence had said Nagumo had in his fleet. Fletcher had no intention of launching all of his airplanes, along with those of *Enterprise* and *Hornet*, against two carriers, only to find himself totally vulnerable to a massive air strike from the two or more as yet unlocated enemy flattops. He also wished to recover the ten scouting airplanes sent out earlier. Realizing that this would delay action against the two already located enemy carriers, Fletcher flashed Spruance at 0607 to "proceed southwesterly and attack enemy

carriers when definitely located. I will follow as soon as my planes are recovered."

Turning to their new course, *Enterprise* and *Hornet* increased speed to 25kts and headed toward Nagumo's presumed position in a bid to close the distance before launching. From the hangar levels the lifts rapidly brought onto their flight decks the SBDs, TBDs and F4Fs with which the two carrier air groups were shortly to launch their strikes. The two carriers then separated, dividing the screening vessels between them to provide air defense if attacked. Spruance now ordered both carriers turned into the wind, and at 0700 *Hornet* started the launching of the 60 aircraft of her strike group. Under her air group leader, Commander Stanhope C. Ring, were the fifteen Devastators of VT-8 led by Lt. Commander John C. Waldron, known as much for his flying and leadership skill as his somewhat idiosyncratic behavior. Thirty-five Dauntless dive-bombers of VB-8 and VS-8, each armed with a 1,000lb bomb in the former unit and a 500lb bomb in the latter, were provided with an escort of just ten Wildcat fighters from VF-8 led by the fighter group commander, Lt. Commander Samuel G. Mitchell.

As *Hornet*'s aircraft assembled they were joined by those from *Enterprise*'s air group, which commenced launching at 0706. The composition of the 61-aircraft group was almost identical to that from *Hornet*. The fourteen torpedo bombers of VT-6 were led by Lt. Commander Eugene E. Lindsey, and the 37 Dauntless dive-bombers of VB-8 and VS-8 were commanded by Lts. Best and Gallaher. Fighter cover was provided by ten Wildcats from VF-6 under the command of Lt. James S. Gray. Spruance's provision of only twenty Wildcats for fighter cover for such a large striking force was governed by caution in protecting his flattops. Ever mindful of Nimitz's charge to preserve the carriers, he had retained 36 Wildcats on *Enterprise* and *Hornet* as fighter cover in the event of a Japanese counterstrike.

In the meantime, having recovered his scouting airplanes, Fletcher increased his speed to 25kts and headed toward Task Force 16. Upon further reflection he had decided that, although just two carriers had been identified so far, they provided too good an opportunity to miss, so he too would launch. However, he allocated only half of *Yorktown*'s air

▶ *Commissioned on 20 October 1941 as the last of the class, USS* **Hornet** *had a short, albeit dramatic, career. Following Midway she met her end on 26 October 1942 during the Battle of Santa Cruz. (via Roger Chesneau*

group to the planned strike, the other half being retained to form a small second strike force. Shortly after 0830 *Yorktown* turned into the wind and began launching seventeen Dauntless of VB-3 under the command of Lt. Commander Maxwell F. Leslie. These were then joined by the twelve Devastators of VT-3 led by Lt. Commander Lance E. Massey and a minimal force of six Wildcats from Fighting Squadron 3. Thus by 0910 Fletcher and Spruance had a total of 156 aircraft airborne and heading for the presumed position of Nagumo's fleet.

### First Air Fleet: 0700–0920

With the scouting airplanes launched, the Japanese carriers were busy once more as the second wave

was brought up from the hangar levels and onto the decks. Comprising 108 aircraft, all crewed by battle proven veterans, the force was under the command of Lt. Commander Takashige Egusa of *Soryu*, regarded by many as the *Rengo Kantai*'s leading exponent of dive-bombing. Thirty-six D3A1s were spotted on the decks of *Soryu* and *Hiryu*, while eighteen "Kates," each loaded with a 24in torpedo, were aboard the *Akagi* and *Kaga* under the command of Lt. Commander Shigeharu Murata. Fighter cover for the whole group was to be provided by 36 "Zeros" commanded by Lt. Commander Shigeru Itaya, also of *Akagi*. Although they were provisionally tasked with the role of attacking any American carrier fleet spotted by the scout aircraft, the lack of any reported sightings as the hours rolled

▶ *Although it depicts a Grumman F4F-3 Wildcat (F4F-4s were flown at Midway) this picture is notable because the machine in the foreground is being flown by Lt Commander "Jimmy" Thach, who commanded* **Yorktown's** *fighters at Midway. (U.S. Navy)*

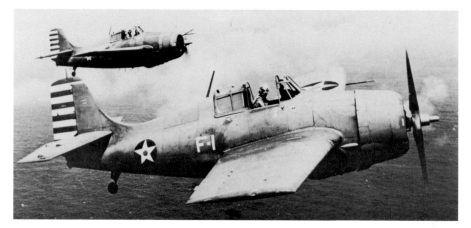

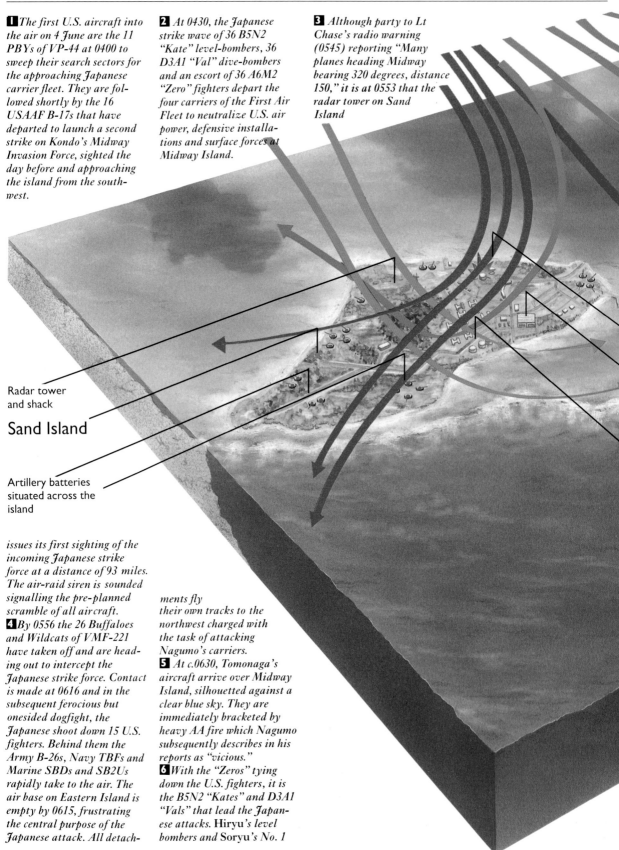

**1** *The first U.S. aircraft into the air on 4 June are the 11 PBYs of VP-44 at 0400 to sweep their search sectors for the approaching Japanese carrier fleet. They are followed shortly by the 16 USAAF B-17s that have departed to launch a second strike on Kondo's Midway Invasion Force, sighted the day before and approaching the island from the southwest.*

**2** *At 0430, the Japanese strike wave of 36 B5N2 "Kate" level-bombers, 36 D3A1 "Val" dive-bombers and an escort of 36 A6M2 "Zero" fighters depart the four carriers of the First Air Fleet to neutralize U.S. air power, defensive installations and surface forces at Midway Island.*

**3** *Although party to Lt Chase's radio warning (0545) reporting "Many planes heading Midway bearing 320 degrees, distance 150," it is at 0553 that the radar tower on Sand Island*

Radar tower
and shack

## Sand Island

Artillery batteries
situated across the
island

*issues its first sighting of the incoming Japanese strike force at a distance of 93 miles. The air-raid siren is sounded signalling the pre-planned scramble of all aircraft.*
**4** *By 0556 the 26 Buffaloes and Wildcats of VMF-221 have taken off and are heading out to intercept the Japanese strike force. Contact is made at 0616 and in the subsequent ferocious but onesided dogfight, the Japanese shoot down 15 U.S. fighters. Behind them the Army B-26s, Navy TBFs and Marine SBDs and SB2Us rapidly take to the air. The air base on Eastern Island is empty by 0615, frustrating the central purpose of the Japanese attack. All detach-*

*ments fly their own tracks to the northwest charged with the task of attacking Nagumo's carriers.*
**5** *At c.0630, Tomonaga's aircraft arrive over Midway Island, silhouetted against a clear blue sky. They are immediately bracketed by heavy AA fire which Nagumo subsequently describes in his reports as "vicious."*
**6** *With the "Zeros" tying down the U.S. fighters, it is the B5N2 "Kates" and D3A1 "Vals" that lead the Japanese attacks.* **Hiryu's** *level bombers and* **Soryu's** *No. 1*

# THE MIDWAY ATTACK

## The Japanese air strikes on the island of Midway, 0400 to 0643 hours, 4 June 1942

*Key*
*BLUE: 36 A6M2 Zero fighters – 9 from each carrier*
*RED: 36 B5N2 "Kate" level-bombers from Soryu and Hiryu – each carrying one 800kg bomb*
*GREEN: 36 D3A1 "Vals" from Akagi and Kaga – each carrying one 250kg bomb*

Main Hangar

Command post
Marine Air Group
22 (MAG-22)

Power
house

Eastern Island

Artillery batteries
situated across the
island

Fuel tanks

Seaplane
base

Fuel tanks

*Squadron concentrates on Sand Island where they are first tasked with the suppression of the AA defenses. Level bombers from Hiryu also set fire to the three fuel tanks on*

*the northeast of Sand Island, causing them to burn out of control for two days. Other damage includes destruction of the hospital, a seaplane hangar and other sundry buildings.*
**7** *The bulk of* Akagi *and* Kaga's *dive-bombers and* Soryu's *No. 2 "Kate" Squadron make for Eastern*

Island *to destroy the hangars presumed to contain aircraft and supporting installations dotted around the air base. All Japanese bombs fall to the north of No. 2 runway, which parallels the southern coastline. The destruction of the main hangar is caught on celluloid by the film director John Ford, who later incorporates the scene into his Oscar-winning film, "The Battle of Midway." Subse-*

*quently another "Val" scores a direct hit on the power house. The rupturing of fuel lines in the dock area means that returning aircraft must be refueled by hand. "Zeros" over both islands strafe AA batteries and targets of opportunity.*
**8** *At 0641 Nagumo receives the message from Tomonaga that the raid has been completed. But two minutes after the raid commander's message that a second raid is needed, Nagumo receives ample confirmation of the obvious failure of the first when U.S. aircraft, launched from Midway over an hour before begin their first attacks on his fleet.*

▲ *These SBD Dauntless dive-bombers are shown spotted on the deck of a carrier while refueling and rearming prior to launch. The Dauntless* *was the standard U.S. Navy dive-bomber and carrier scouting type at the time of Midway. (Philip Jarrett)*

by served only to confirm the presumptions of senior officers and aircrew alike that the Americans were not out there at all. It is not surprising, therefore, that, when Nagumo received Tomonaga's 0700 signal requesting a second strike on Midway, he pondered its content with a degree of sympathy that, within minutes, hardened to firm assent as the first U.S. aircraft dispatched from the atoll base barely an hour before began their attack on the First Air Fleet.

Approaching the Japanese carriers were the four B–26s under the command of Captain James F. Collins and the six TBFs of VT–8 led by Lt. Langdon K. Fieberling. Lookouts on *Akagi* were the first to track the incoming hostiles, and within minutes her speed increased as the ship and her screening

vessels turned to face the attackers, thereby offering them the smallest possible target. Exploding shells and smoke bursts attended the passage of the enemy airplanes as the screening destroyers and the heavy cruiser *Tone* added to the barrage of antiaircraft fire erupting from *Akagi*'s batteries. Behind this curtain of fire, ten of Itaya's "Zeros" had been sent aloft to join those of the standing air patrol. These rapidly hauled around behind the attackers and soon started wreaking havoc among the incoming aircraft.

The TBFs came in first, their speed much reduced owing to the need to open their bomb bay doors to launch their torpedoes. Maintaining course despite the hail of antiaircraft fire to their front and the attacking "Zeros" to their rear, they managed to loose off several torpedoes mainly directed at *Akagi*, which was able to avoid them by deft maneuvering. Of the TBFs that flew in low to attack the carriers, five were brought down. Only one escaped to limp back to Midway, its hydraulic system shot up, its controls badly damaged and the rear gunner dead in his turret. The B–26s followed, skimming just above the wave tops with the ever present "Zeros" snapping at their heels. One was destroyed on the run, disintegrating into a thousand pieces as it hit the sea at nearly 200mph. Fuchida clearly recalled seeing another of the bombers, the white star on its fuselage clearly visible, skimming low over the *Akagi* and barely missing its bridge before bursting into flames and crashing into the sea beyond. The two remaining Marauders, including the one flown by Collins, managed to drop their torpedoes and survived the barrage of fire thrown up by the Japanese vessels to return to Midway.

This attack swung the decision for Nagumo. He could hardly retain his second strike force to counter a nonexistent threat when a real and very tangible one, in the form of Midway's as yet undestroyed air power, did exist. He snappily ordered that the airplanes of the second wave be prepared to attack Midway. That meant a rapid disarming of the "Kates" on board *Akagi* and *Kaga*, to replace their torpedoes with bombs. Frantically, the deck crews on the two vessels hauled the airplanes to the lifts, from whence they were taken down to the hangar levels. Here sweating armorers worked as quickly as possible to change the armament so that the aircraft could be returned topside. Even under normal conditions it took the best part of an hour to carry out this procedure.

As Nagumo and his bridge staff were no doubt convinced of the logic of his decision, it must have

come as no small shock to them when, 25 minutes later, they were presented with a splendidly vague message from *Tone*'s Number Four floatplane. It read: "Sight what appears to be 10 enemy surface ships, in position 10 degrees distance 240 miles from Midway. Course 150 speed over 20 knots." Minoru Genda observed that the fact and imprecision of the sighting left Nagumo and his staff unable to make an accurate judgment of the situation and how best to respond. The admiral was indeed in a quandary. While his original orders called for the neutralization of Midway's air power, he clearly could not ignore the potential danger to his own fleet implied by the sighting of these U.S. naval vessels, whatever their type. Furthermore, the aircraft of Tomonaga's strike group were on their way back to the carriers and they would need to land, refuel and rearm, even though aircraft of the second wave were still spotted on the carrier decks. Pondering his options, Nagumo signaled his commanders at 0745 that he had decided to continue preparing for the second strike on Midway, but ordered that those bombers whose armament was as yet unchanged retain their torpedoes, so as to be able to "carry out attacks on enemy fleet units."

A few minutes later *Akagi* signaled the pilot of *Tone*'s Number Four aircraft with a curt injunction to "Ascertain ship types, and maintain contact." All now turned on the identity of the vessels and the dispatch with which any new sighting was sent to

▶ *By the time of the Battle of Midway, the TBD Devastator torpedo bomber was decidedly obsolescent. Its slow speed and poor rate of climb made it a sitting duck for Japanese "Zero-Sen" fighters. Those shown here are from VT-6, and the prewar picture dates from 1939, when the planes were resplendent with chrome yellow wings and blue tails. (via Robert F. Dorr)*

*Sweeping all before it in the first months of the war, the A6M2 "Zero" was still the finest carrier fighter in the world at Midway. (Pilot Press copyright drawing)*

the flagship. If no carrier was detected among them, and they proved only to be surface warships, Nagumo believed he had the time to realize the best of both worlds – launch the second wave against Midway and then recover the returning first strike force. Once they were refueled and rearmed, Tomonaga's airplanes could be launched again, this time to strike at the American vessels. Barely had the Admiral and his staff finished reflecting on their options when, at 0748, a signal from *Soryu* drew their attention to the beginning of yet another air attack on the fleet.

The incoming aircraft on this occasion were the sixteen Dauntlesses of VMSB-241, but their passage toward the carriers was hampered from an early stage by the dogged attention of a swarm of "Zeros." Fuchida, watching events from the deck of *Akagi*, expressed surprise that the airplanes were employing a low-angle glide attack and not the "hell-diving" technique that was their forte. He could not know that Major Lofton Henderson, who was commanding the incoming aircraft, had good reason for choosing this tactic, deeming it to be the only one he could realistically employ because most of the young and very green pilots he was leading had almost no experience at the controls of an SBD. The low-angle approach with dive brakes deployed made them easy targets for the "Zeros," and even

◀ *As part of the air search pattern instigated by Nagumo after the launch of the Midway strike force, the battleship* **Haruna** *catapulted its old and short-ranged Nakajima E8N "Dave" floatplane to survey to the north of the southward-moving carrier fleet. (Philip Jarrett)*

*Although inferior to the Zero in many respects, the Grumman F4F Wildcat nevertheless proved a remarkably rugged and effective aircraft. (Pilot Press copyright drawing)*

before they reached the fleet half of their number had been shot down. Seemingly oblivious to the fate of their comrades, the remainder doggedly held their course even as they flew into the curtain of antiaircraft fire thrown up by the now rapidly maneuvering warships. At the end of their glide attacks the SBDs released their bombs, most of which were targeted at the *Hiryu*. To observers on the other ships of the fleet it seemed as if the carrier must be hit, as she disappeared behind a wall of water plumes and smoke. Within minutes she emerged, clearly unscathed by the experience.

As the eight surviving SBDs made their escape by flying low across the sea, pursued by the fighters,

the pressure on the Japanese was relentlessly maintained. High overhead Lt. Colonel Sweeney's Flying Fortresses swung into view. From 20,000ft the B-17s dropped their loads of 500lb bombs on their targets four miles below. As on the previous day, the dramatic view of bombs bursting close to enemy vessels led the Army pilots to claim heavy damage on the Japanese carriers, although none was actually hit.

At 0806 Nagumo received the response he had been awaiting from *Tone*'s Number Four scout. Its content could hardly have carried better tidings for the harassed admiral: "Enemy is composed of 5 cruisers and 5 destroyers." Nevertheless Kusaka, the

▶ *Delays in launching the Mitsubishi Type "O" "Pete" observer floatplanes from the heavy cruiser* **Tone,** *and engine problems with that from* **Chikuna,** *were to deny the Japanese the intelligence of the approach of the U.S. Task Forces from the east. (Philip Jarrett)*

*◄ Six crews of VT-8 had the distinction of taking the new Grumman TBF-1 into combat at Midway. Only one of the airplanes survived the attack on the carriers to return, badly shot up, to Midway, where its undercarriage collapsed on landing. The aircraft was thereafter named "Avenger" in memory of the five crews that did not return. (U.S. Navy)*

Chief of Staff of the First Air Fleet, was of the opinion that a force so constituted would hardly be at sea unless there was a carrier present. Notwithstanding his eminently reasonable deduction, there can be no doubting the very genuine sense of relief fostered by the 0806 message, for as matters now stood the second strike on Midway could proceed. Even a further attack by Midway-based Marine Vindicators after 0820 did nothing to dampen the spirits of Nagumo and his staff. They were not to know that, with the departure of Major Norris's surviving SB2Us, land-based air power from Midway had shot its bolt. The results of the combat thus far had been totally in favor of the Japanese. From 0702 until 0830 they had been attacked by 131 aircraft, with numerous U.S. aircraft shot down for no registered hits on any vessels of the First Air Fleet. Fuchida remarked that, in his opinion, the U.S. flyers had not displayed a high level of ability, a view shared on the bridge of *Akagi*. The prevailing sentiment was that, if this was the best the enemy could throw at them, the Japanese had little to fear.

Into this self-congratulatory atmosphere on the bridge of *Akagi* the latest message from Scout Number Four dropped like a bombshell on Nagumo and his staff officers at 0830: "The enemy is accompanied by what appears to be a carrier in a position to the rear of the others." All were momentarily shocked at the news, and it could not have come at a worse moment. For accompanying Nagumo's receipt of this message came the first sighting of Tomonaga's returning airplanes. Many of the aircraft were low on fuel or damaged, and on arrival

over the fleet they began to circle as they awaited permission to land. Unless the decks of the carriers were rapidly cleared of the second strike wave the returning aircraft would have no alternative but to ditch in the sea. Speed of decision was therefore of the essence. No discussion was needed for the planned second strike on Midway to be aborted. It was self-evident to all on *Akagi*'s bridge that the American carrier now posed the greater danger and must take first priority.

Herein lay the dilemma for Nagumo. Of the bombers in the second strike wave, the bulk of the "Kates" were armed with bombs and not with the more efficacious torpedoes. Should they be launched as armed against the carrier? Certainly Admiral Yamaguchi on *Hiryu* believed so, and signaled Nagumo to that effect. But Nagumo knew that to launch the strike aircraft immediately would be to do so without benefit of fighter cover. Itaya's "Zeros" had been aloft since early morning, helping the small number of fighters of the fleet combat air patrol defeat the repeated U.S. air attacks. They were also waiting in the circuit to land to refuel and rearm. Nagumo was acutely conscious of the questionable value of sending out the bombers without fighter cover, as they would prove highly vulnerable to interception by enemy fighters – a point well made by the Japanese themselves in the previous few hours. He therefore believed he had sound reasons for supposing that a strike dispatched immediately would prove to be of dubious value and lead only to the loss of valuable men and machines.

Genda and Kusaka were also fully cognizant of these matters, and were prompted in consequence to advise Nagumo to recover Tomonaga's force first, and only then attack the carrier. That would require the second-strike aircraft at present spotted on the decks to be taken down to the hangar levels to clear the decks. While that was being done, the "Kates" could then also be rearmed with torpedoes. it could not be said that Nagumo suffered from any agony of indecision on this occasion. Less than two minutes elapsed from his receipt of the scout airplane's message to the fateful signal flashed to all carriers, instructing that the Midway attackers be allowed to land and the second-wave strike bombers be rearmed with torpedoes. This

was followed at 0835 by a further signal, ordering that once all aircraft had been recovered, the whole fleet would turn north to "contact and destroy the enemy force."

As the gongs sounded and orders were barked across the flight decks there was an intense flurry of activity on all four carriers as aircraft were manhandled to the lifts and then taken down to the hangar levels. Within minutes they were clear and at 0837 the first of Tomonaga's thirsty charges touched down. On board *Kaga* and *Akagi* sweating armorers once more lowered bombs from shackles and began the laborious and tiring work of reloading the torpedoes. Owing to the pressure of time and the constant demands of officers to speed up the process, safety procedures were ignored as bombs were casually stacked en masse at the sides of the hangars. To acquire a better fix on the American vessels, more scout airplanes were launched at about 0845, including one of the new D4Ys from *Soryu*. Scout airplane Number Four then came back on the air to inform *Tone*'s captain that he was returning to the ship as, having been airborne since 0500, he was running low on fuel. He was immediately told to postpone and turn on his DF transmitter to allow the carrier fleet to home in on his position.

With the last of the Midway attackers and Itaya's "Zeros" recovered by 0917, the whole fleet changed course. A shudder was felt throughout *Akagi* as speed was increased to 30kts, and along with the other carriers the fleet turned to its new heading of

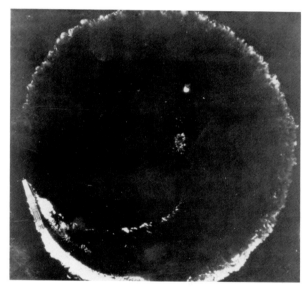

▲ *The* Soryu *makes nearly a full turn as it seeks to evade the bombs from Lieutenant Colonel Sweeney's B-17s which arrived over the Japanese carriers shortly after 0800. (U.S. National Archives)*

▶ *Of the nine slow and venerable Vought SB2U-3 Vindicators – nicknamed "Vibrators" by their crews – that left Midway to attack Nagumo's carriers, two were shot down. (Philip Jarrett)*

◄ *An unusual view of* **Akagi**'s *flight deck, as seen from the gunner's position in a "Kate" bomber that has just launched. Of note is the island offset to port, a feature found on only one other carrier ever built – the* **Hiryu**. *Note the Imperial symbol of the gold chrysanthemum carried on her bow and on all other warships of the Rengo Kantai.*

◄ *Although another pre-Pearl Harbor photograph, it is nevertheless of interest showing* **Hiryu** *viewed from the rear flight deck of her consort* **Soryu**, *on which "Val" dive-bombers are warming up for takeoff.*

0430: Japanese first strike wave launched against Midway Island

0545: PBY sigh Nagumo's carri

Midway Strike Force TOMO
A6M+B5N+D3A1

Midwa
Occupati
Force

# Operations on 4 June 1942

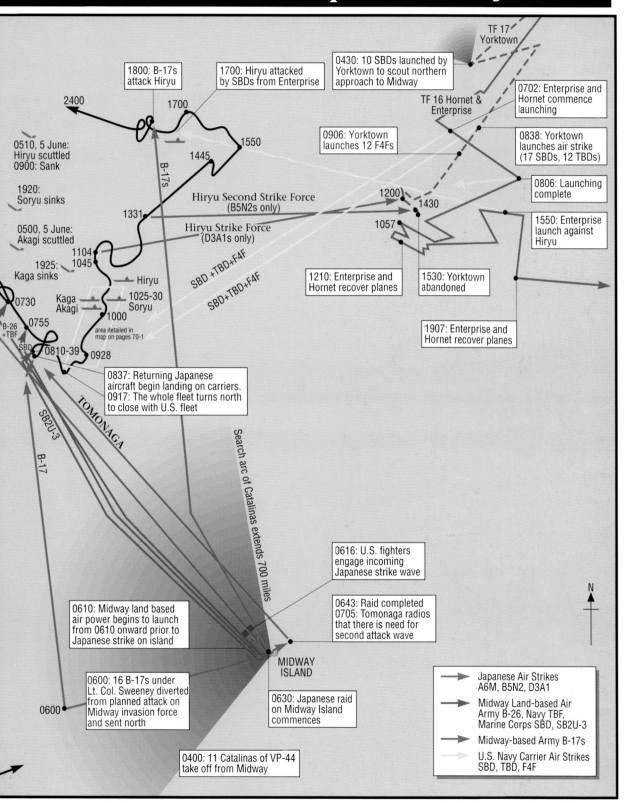

TF 17 Yorktown

**0430:** 10 SBDs launched by Yorktown to scout northern approach to Midway

TF 16 Hornet & Enterprise

**0702:** Enterprise and Hornet commence launching

**1800:** B-17s attack Hiryu

**1700:** Hiryu attacked by SBDs from Enterprise

2400

1700

**0906:** Yorktown launches 12 F4Fs

**0838:** Yorktown launches air strike (17 SBDs, 12 TBDs)

1550

**0510, 5 June:** Hiryu scuttled
**0900:** Sank

1445

B-17s

**0806:** Launching complete

**1920:** Soryu sinks

1200

1430

**1550:** Enterprise launch against Hiryu

Hiryu Second Strike Force (B5N2s only)

1331

1057

**0500, 5 June:** Akagi scuttled

Hiryu Strike Force (D3A1s only)

SBD +TBD+F4F

**1210:** Enterprise and Hornet recover planes

**1530:** Yorktown abandoned

1104
1045

**1925:** Kaga sinks

Hiryu

SBD+TBD+F4F

1025-30
Soryu

**0730**

Kaga
Akagi

1000

**1907:** Enterprise and Hornet recover planes

B-26 +TBF

**0755**

area detailed in map on pages 70-1

SBD

**0810-39**

0928

**0837:** Returning Japanese aircraft begin landing on carriers.
**0917:** The whole fleet turns north to close with U.S. fleet

TOMONAGA

SB2U-3

B-17

**0616:** U.S. fighters engage incoming Japanese strike wave

Search arc of Catalinas extends 700 miles

**0643:** Raid completed
**0705:** Tomonaga radios that there is need for second attack wave

**0610:** Midway land based air power begins to launch from 0610 onward prior to Japanese strike on island

MIDWAY ISLAND

N

**0600:** 16 B-17s under Lt. Col. Sweeney diverted from planned attack on Midway invasion force and sent north

**0630:** Japanese raid on Midway Island commences

**0600**

**0400:** 11 Catalinas of VP-44 take off from Midway

Japanese Air Strikes
A6M, B5N2, D3A1

Midway Land-based Air Army B-26, Navy TBF, Marine Corps SBD, SB2U-3

Midway-based Army B-17s

U.S. Navy Carrier Air Strikes SBD, TBD, F4F

◀ *Of the 63 aircraft carried by* **Akagi** *at Midway, 21 were Nakajima B5N2 "Kate" bombers. However, in the strike wave launched against Midway Island, the "Kates" were employed as level bombers substituting an 800kg bomb for the 24in aerial torpedo normally carried.*

east-northeast in a bid to close the distance to the American force. Nagumo was confident of being well placed to launch his first strike, comprising 102 aircraft, against the American carrier by 1030. The question on everyone's mind was, would they be given the time, or would the Americans strike first? Anxious eyes swept the sky for the air strike that all aboard had been expecting ever since the American carrier was sighted. Barely three minutes later, keen eyes peering through binoculars aboard *Chikuma* spotted a collection of black dots on the horizon; they were growing larger by the moment. So, there they were!

Nevertheless, optimism continued to reign on the bridge of *Akagi* and throughout the fleet, for all believed that this attack would be weathered as easily as had the others earlier in the morning. But as the American aircraft tracked in toward the fleet, this confidence proceeded to dissipate rapidly. With each sighting it became increasingly apparent to Nagumo and his staff that there were far too many inbound hostiles to have come from just one enemy carrier. Orders were hastily issued to speed up the preparations for launching the air strike, but it was already too late. The U.S. Navy flyers had caught the four Japanese carriers at their most vulnerable, and in just the situation that Spruance had hoped for – in the midst of refueling and rearming their aircraft. Unbeknown to Nagumo, the fate of the carriers, their airplanes and their pilots was already sealed. The life of the seemingly invincible First Carrier Strike Force had but one hour to run.

## The Courageous Sacrifice

Spruance had intended to have all the aircraft of Task Force 16's Striking Force assemble in one large formation before heading off to attack Nagumo's carriers. To that end the SBDs were launched first, as with their greater range they could afford to circle the Task Force, burning fuel while the shorter-legged Wildcats and Devastators took off and joined the formation. But the discovery of *Tone*'s scout airplane hovering on the horizon prompted him to change his mind. Fearing that the strike force would lose its element of surprise, Spruance ordered Lt. Commander Wade McClusky, already aloft with his 33 SBDs, to depart immediately, leaving the torpedo bombers and fighters to follow. Although McClusky was thus deprived of any fighter cover, it was clear that the Wildcats would be needed to protect the lumbering and highly vulnerable TBDs.

Shortly before 0800 McClusky turned southeast, heading toward the assumed position of Nagumo's force. He was followed by *Hornet*'s dive-bombers and fighters and Waldron's VT-8. As the aircraft of *Hornet*'s strike group took their leave, *Enterprise*'s Wildcats were circling the carrier, waiting for the last of the TBDs of VT-6 to take to the air. With their departure the strike force had become spread out into four distinct bodies: McClusky's SBDs, *Hornet*'s SBDs and F4Fs, and the two torpedo bombing squadrons. In addition, the onset of layers of broken cloud made it increasingly difficult for the dive-bombers and fighters flying at 19,000ft to observe the torpedo bombers, which were holding course just

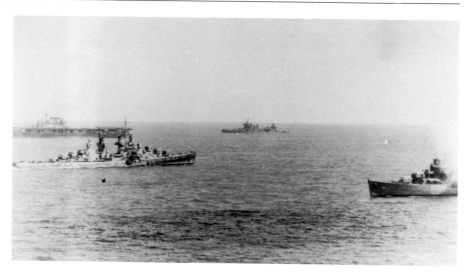

► *Seen here early on 4 June is the USS* Hornet *and her attendant screening vessels comprising the light cruiser* Atlanta *on the left, a* New Orleans-*class heavy cruiser midfield, and the destroyer* Phelps. *(via Robert C. Stern)*

above the wavetops. The Wildcats of VF-6 had been tasked with protecting VT-6, but in the confusion caused by the cloud cover Lt. Gray had unknowingly lost track of VT-6, and ended up flying top cover to Waldron's VT-8. Waldron did not know of the pre-arranged signal whereby Gray's fighters would descend to aid VT-6, and in consequence both squadrons of torpedo bombers ended up attacking the Japanese carriers devoid of fighter support.

At the time of the launch neither Spruance nor Fletcher had received any update on the position of Nagumo's force since their receipt of Ady's original sighting report. They were therefore totally unaware of Nagumo's change of course away from Midway and his subsequent run to the north to close with the American carrier group. Thus Task Force 16's attack force had struck out on a direct route toward the estimated position of Nagumo's carriers, on the erroneous assumption he was still holding his southeasterly course toward Midway. Anticipating that contact would be made with the enemy between 0915 and 0939, *Hornet*'s dive-bombers and fighters arrived in position only to find themselves over a wide and empty expanse of the Pacific. Choosing to hold this same course, Ring then decided – wrongly, as it transpired – that Nagumo must have moved even further south

toward Midway. Consequently, the SBDs and F4Fs of *Hornet*'s Air Group were drawn even further away from Nagumo's actual position. Unable to locate the Japanese fleet, and with fuel running low, Ring led some of the SBDs back to the carrier while others landed on Midway. The Wildcats, however, were forced to ditch as, one after another, their fuel tanks ran dry.

Following his own hunch, Waldron led his squadron for only part of the way along the identified route before changing course and heading northwest. In his final briefing to his men he had confided in them that he believed that, once Nagumo became aware of the presence of the American carriers, he would change his course and heading.

► *Lieutenant Commander John C. Waldron was squadron commander of VT-8 aboard* Hornet, *and led the first of the attacks by the carrier-based aircraft on the Japanese Fleet. All 15 of Waldron's aircraft were shot down. (U.S. National Archives)*

# The Carrier Air Strikes on Nagumo's Carriers, 0920-1200

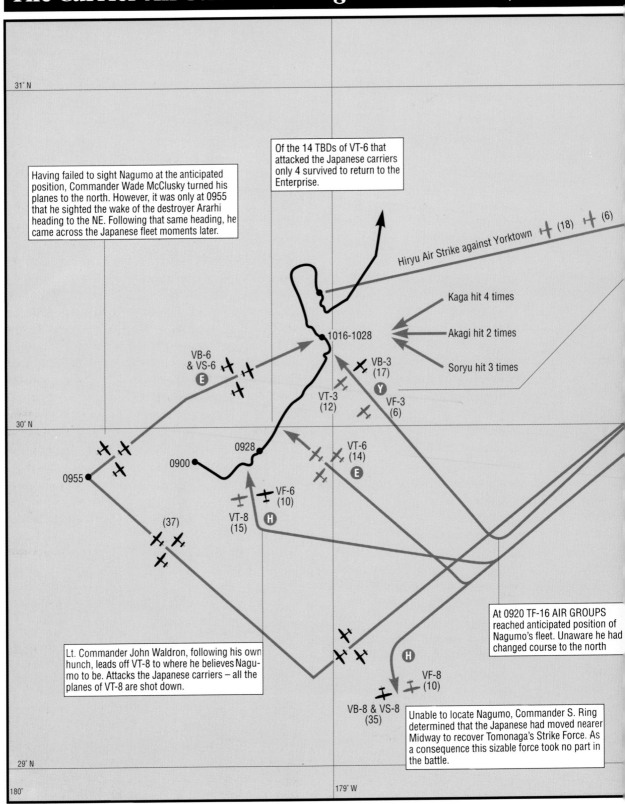

Having failed to sight Nagumo at the anticipated position, Commander Wade McClusky turned his planes to the north. However, it was only at 0955 that he sighted the wake of the destroyer Ararhi heading to the NE. Following that same heading, he came across the Japanese fleet moments later.

Of the 14 TBDs of VT-6 that attacked the Japanese carriers only 4 survived to return to the Enterprise.

Hiryu Air Strike against Yorktown (18) (6)

Kaga hit 4 times

Akagi hit 2 times

Soryu hit 3 times

VB-6 & VS-6 E

1016-1028

VB-3 (17) Y

VT-3 (12)

VF-3 (6)

0928

VT-6 (14) E

0900

0955 (37)

VF-6 (10)

VT-8 (15) H

Lt. Commander John Waldron, following his own hunch, leads off VT-8 to where he believes Nagumo to be. Attacks the Japanese carriers – all the planes of VT-8 are shot down.

At 0920 TF-16 AIR GROUPS reached anticipated position of Nagumo's fleet. Unaware he had changed course to the north

VF-8 (10) H

VB-8 & VS-8 (35)

Unable to locate Nagumo, Commander S. Ring determined that the Japanese had moved nearer Midway to recover Tomonaga's Strike Force. As a consequence this sizable force took no part in the battle.

31° N

30° N

29° N

180°

179° W

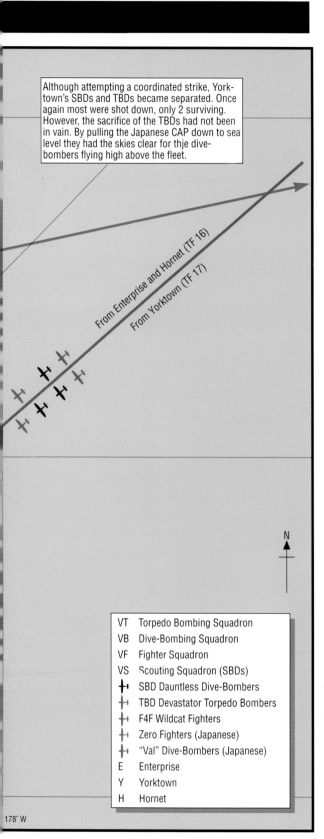

Although attempting a coordinated strike, Yorktown's SBDs and TBDs became separated. Once again most were shot down, only 2 surviving. However, the sacrifice of the TBDs had not been in vain. By pulling the Japanese CAP down to sea level they had the skies clear for thje dive-bombers flying high above the fleet.

From Enterprise and Hornet (TF 16)

From Yorktown (TF 17)

N

| VT | Torpedo Bombing Squadron |
|---|---|
| VB | Dive-Bombing Squadron |
| VF | Fighter Squadron |
| VS | Scouting Squadron (SBDs) |
| ✈ | SBD Dauntless Dive-Bombers |
| ✈ | TBD Devastator Torpedo Bombers |
| ✈ | F4F Wildcat Fighters |
| ✈ | Zero Fighters (Japanese) |
| ✈ | "Val" Dive-Bombers (Japanese) |
| E | Enterprise |
| Y | Yorktown |
| H | Hornet |

178° W

He said that he would do the same, and told his men to follow him as he knew where he was going. Waldron was under no illusions about the prospects of survival for his squadron, but told them that if only one of them survived the run-in, he wanted him to go in and get a hit. Flying his squadron as straight as a die, Waldron found the Japanese Fleet exactly where he believed it would be. At 0920 the fifteen Devastators of VT-8 began their lone and suicidal assault on the enemy fleet.

As Nagumo's command accelerated on to its new heading its vessels deployed to provide maximum defensive coverage for the carriers in the event of air attack. In the van of the advancing fleet the light cruiser *Nagara* shepherded the destroyers which screened the advancing fleet to its fore and flanks. To the rear of *Nagara*, sailing in line ahead, were the fast battleships *Kirishima* and *Haruna*, flanked to port and starboard by the carriers *Akagi* and *Hiryu* and *Kaga* and *Soryu* respectively. The battleships were so placed to bring to bear the firepower of their heavy antiaircraft batteries in defense of the carriers. The heavy cruisers *Tone* and *Chikuma* provided flank cover for the inner group of warships and the outermost antiaircraft screen. No fewer than 50 "Zeros" were aloft to provide a comprehensive standing air patrol. As soon as Waldron's squadron was spotted at 0920 the fighters veered off and accelerated toward the incoming torpedo bombers.

Waggling his wings, Waldron signaled his squadron to begin their attack. As he was unable to call down Gray's Wildcats circling uselessly above him at 20,000ft, his attack went in without fighter cover. It seems that he intended to target *Akagi*, but

◄ *Just five minutes was sufficient for the balance of naval power in the Pacific to be changed forever. Between 1020 and 1025 on the morning of 4 June 1942, the dive-bombers of Task Forces 16 and 17 destroyed three of Admiral Nagumo's carriers.* Hiryu *followed later that day. In one fell swoop the U.S. Navy Dauntlesses had eliminated an*

*overwhelming Japanese superiority in naval air power, the vital key to the successful prosecution of war in the vast expanse of the Pacific theater. Those five minutes transformed an empire at the zenith of its power into one facing the prospect of defeat and inevitable ruin. The battle of Midway is for that reason one of the most decisive battles ever fought.*

◀ *The pilots of VT-8 pose for the camera aboard* Hornet *shortly before their fatal attack on the Japanese carriers at Midway. Only Ensign George Gay, fourth from the left in the front row, survived the attack. Clutching a piece of wreckage, he witnessed the rest of the battle from the water. (U.S. Navy)*

eight miles out from the fleet the first of the "Zeros" swept down on the low-flying squadron and began hacking the TBDs from the air in a hail of machine gun and cannon fire. Within seconds they had accounted for four of them. As the survivors flew ever nearer they encountered a wall of antiaircraft fire that tore apart the airframes and killed the crews. Fuchida, who was watching from the flagship, recounted how "occasionally one of the specks burst into a spark of flame and trailed black smoke as it fell into the water." Although all of the TBDs were lost, there was one survivor. Ensign George Gay, who was flying in the last of the Devastators, later recounted how, as he flew through the flak and toward *Akagi*, he heard his gunner cry out as he was killed by fire from the "Zeros" on his tail. Even though he had been wounded by a 20mm cannon shell in his foot and his airplane had been riddled and holed, he managed to release his torpedo. Pulling up over the carrier, he nearly hit its bridge before the fire from the "Zeros" that were chasing him sent his aircraft crashing into the the sea beyond. Gay managed to abandon his sinking Devastator and, by catching hold of an inflatable life raft, floated free of the wreckage to become an unwitting spectator of the dramatic events of the next few hours.

Even as it was announced that all fifteen of the torpedo bombers had been shot down, the work of preparing the strike force went on. Amid the violent defensive maneuvers aircraft were still being brought up and spotted on deck and having their engines run up. Nagumo now needed a period of rel-

ative calm to enable the airplanes to be launched, but the gallant sacrifice of VT-8 meant that the carrier fleet had been forced to waste vital minutes in defensive action. This delay was further compounded when it was announced that yet another enemy force had been spotted. Inbound to the fleet were Lindsay's fourteen Devastators from VT-6. From *Akagi* it appeared that they were attempting a concerted attack from either bow in single columns.

Although their designated fighter cover was still circling high overhead, Lindsay did not give the signal that would have brought Gray's Wildcats plummeting down on the "Zeros" that were even now tearing into his two columns. As the Devastators bore in toward the fleet, skimming the wave tops, the Japanese fighters began to scythe down the American torpedo bombers. Ripped apart by shellfire, they exploded, disintegrated and fell into the sea. By the time they reached the torpedo release point for *Akagi*, only seven of the bombers were still airborne. For some reason these then peeled away from the flagship and headed instead for the *Hiryu*. Flying through the hail of flak being thrown up by the warships, and pursued by the "Zeros," the seven surviving aircraft launched their torpedoes at Yamaguchi's carrier. By turning hard to port the *Hiryu* succeeded in avoiding them all. As the TBDs pulled away from the fleet a further three were hacked down, only four managing to return to the *Enterprise*.

Hardly had the "Zeros" landed to refuel and rearm when, at 1015, lookouts on the *Akagi* sighted yet another incoming attack of torpedo bombers. Unlike the previous two attacks, *Yorktown*'s contingent of Massey's twelve Devastators had arrived as part of a coherent strike group. In addition to a small fighter force of six Wildcats under Jimmy Thach, high overhead cruised Leslie's seventeen dive bombers. The intention was to launch a combined assault on the Japanese warships in the hope of swamping the defenses, thus increasing the chance of at least some of the aircraft getting through. All was going well as the Americans approached the Japanese force. Visibility was good, for when first spotted, some 40 miles distant, Nagumo's vessels were seen to be maneuvering violently, indicating that they were clearly under attack. But as the *Yorktown*'s group deployed for action, the dive-bombers flew into heavy cloud and radio contact was lost with the TBDs and the F4Fs far below.

For Massey and his eleven charges, what now unfolded was nothing more than a replay of the slaughter of the earlier Devastator attacks. The presence of Thach's Wildcats became somewhat academic. So many "Zeros" were airborne that, once the American fighters were embroiled in a dogfight with some of the Japanese aircraft, more than sufficient were left over to attack Massey's torpedo bombers with impunity. Of the twelve Devastators that began the run-in, only seven were still in the air some minutes later as they reached their final run-in positions to their targets. Two more, including Massey's, blew up as they ran into the hail of fire thrown up by the ships. The remaining five lunged ahead, splitting their attacks on the *Hiryu* and *Kaga*, but in the face of the devastating wall of flak and the omnipresent "Zeros" their torpedoes, once launched, veered wide of their targets. Freed of the weight of their weapons, the surviving TBDs struggled desperately to escape, but two more fell flaming into the sea and another disintegrated as it crossed the outer screen of warships. Only two of VT-3's Devastators returned to land forlornly on *Enterprise*'s deck at 1020.

## Nemesis

There was a grim sense of satisfaction on the bridge of *Akagi* as the last of the TBDs staggered away from the carriers. Once again, wave after wave of American torpedo bombers had been thrown at the First Air Fleet and destroyed with no damage incurred. Now was the moment for the riposte. Without further delay Nagumo ordered all carriers turned into the wind to make ready for launching. Who could doubt that, with the cream of the *Rengo Kantai*'s pilots about to take off from the decks of the four carriers, Japan was on the verge of realizing the decisive victory she so desired? Yet the sacrifice of the 37 American torpedo bombers and their crews had not been in vain. By their repeated attacks the TBD squadrons had thoroughly disrupted the integrity of the defensive screen around Nagumo's carriers. More significantly, their low-level attacks had pulled down the "Zero" fighter screen from medium to high altitude, where they normally patrolled, to sea level. This left the skies above the fleet unprotected and the carriers totally vulnerable to attack from the U.S. dive-bombers hidden in the clouds above. The engines of the strike group on all four carriers rose to a crescendo as pilots eagerly awaited the signal for takeoff. At almost the same moment as Nagumo gave the order to launch the strike force, a lookout on *Kaga* made the first sighting of the plummeting U.S. dive-bombers. The time was 1020.

Overhead were McClusky's and Leslie's SBD squadrons. The former had almost not made it. He had initially proceeded to Nagumo's estimated position but, finding nothing there, chose, unlike Ring, to fly north rather than south. As he had already used up half of his fuel, his decision to proceed was brave, for if the Japanese had not been spotted soon the whole squadron would have had to ditch. Just after 1000 McClusky saw the faint wake of a Japanese destroyer racing to the north. Following the same heading, he was soon rewarded by the sight of three of the carriers under attack. Although Leslie's passage to the fleet had been more direct, it was not without incident. In the process of arming their weapons, faulty electrical circuits caused a number of the SBDs, including Leslie's, to drop their bombs. When both SBD groups finally located the Japanese fleet, Leslie's SBDs approached from the southeast and McClusky's came up from the southwest. Their respective approaches gave the pilots differing perspectives of the positions of the enemy carriers, resulting in a dispute that continues to this day regarding whose airplanes subsequently hit which carriers. This account has no space to investigate the respective claims of either group, but these can be explored by examining a number of the texts in the bibliography. Needless to say, such matters were somewhat academic to those in the Japanese carriers that now became the targets and victims of the U.S. "Helldivers."

Only a few desultory bursts of antiaircraft fire greeted the first of the Dauntlesses as they came hurtling out of the sun. *Kaga* was the first to be struck, the pilots no doubt attracted by her huge size. Four bombs were sufficient to reduce her to a blazing wreck in a matter of minutes. The first three missed her, but the fourth dropped squarely amid the mass of fully armed and fueled aircraft waiting to take off on the rear of her flight deck. In the eruption of fuel and bombs, aircrew were cremated in their cockpits as the flight deck became a massive funeral pyre. Burning fuel seeped from the deck to the lower levels, filling the passageways and cutting off crew members. Two other bombs hit near the forward elevator, one penetrating to the hangar level where aircraft of the second wave were being fueled and armed. The explosion detonated their fuel tanks

and the many 800kg bombs that had been so casually stashed during the first rearming earlier in the morning. The eruption of the high-octane fuel transformed the hangar level into a conflagration, killing the mechanics and armorers at work there. The deck became an inferno when the explosion of the fourth bomb generated a shock wave which ruptured a fuel bowser. This then exploded, killing Captain Okada and his command staff on the bridge.

*Kaga*'s air officer assumed command, but it was clear that the fire-fighting teams were conducting a losing battle, for the ship was now blazing from stem to stern. Antiaircraft guns began firing of their own accord as the ferocious heat set off their magazines. All lights went out as the power failed, and the carrier began to list. For three hours firefighting teams tried to control the flames that were ravaging what was now little more than a blazing hulk. The ship had become so hot that even the paint had begun to burn on what remained of the superstructure. Although many of the crew had already jumped overboard, Captain Amagai did not give the final order to abandon ship until 1640. By this time *Kaga* was alone

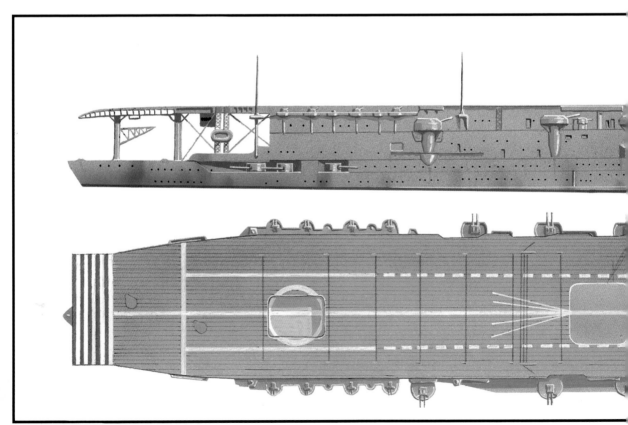

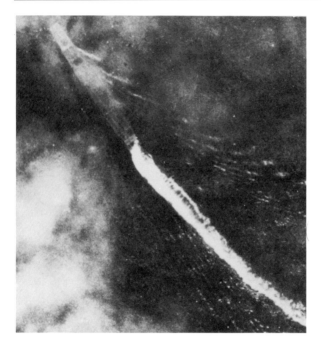

▲ Akagi *prior to being hit by three bombs from SBDs of VF-8 commanded by* *Lieutenant Richard H. Best.* Akagi *was hit at 1026. (U.S. Navy)*

and forlorn, with just the destroyers *Maikaze* and *Hagikaze* picking up survivors. An attack by the U.S. submarine *Nautilus* on the *Kaga* (which was mistaken for the *Soryu*) does not seem to have contributed to her sinking. The end did not come until 1925, when observers saw her hull rent by two massive explosions as the fires reached the magazines. Shortly thereafter the flaming hulk turned over and sank into the deep, taking with her over 800 of her crew and virtually all of her aircraft and aircrew.

A similar fate befell *Akagi*. The first "Zero" was already beginning its takeoff run when three SBDs were seen plummeting toward the flagship. The first released its bomb at 2,500ft, but this missed the ship and fell into the sea on the starboard side. The second hit the target, exploding close to the rear lift and twisting it so badly that it fell into the hangar below. The third fell among the packed aircraft waiting to take off on the rear of the deck. These erupted and flared in a sheet of burning fuel and exploding bombs, incinerating the élite of the Air Fleet where they sat. The rear of the carrier was transformed into an inferno likened by

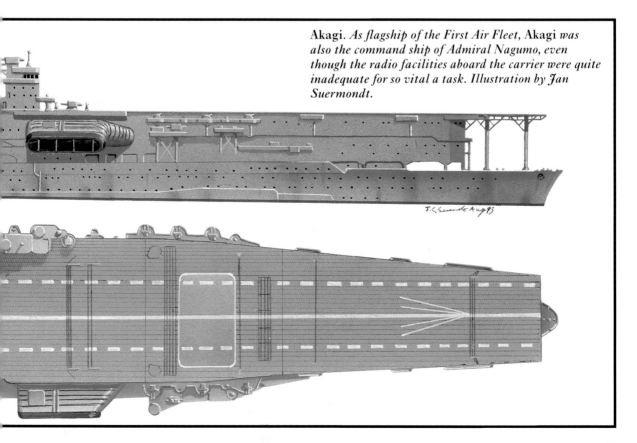

Akagi. *As flagship of the First Air Fleet,* Akagi *was also the command ship of Admiral Nagumo, even though the radio facilities aboard the carrier were quite inadequate for so vital a task. Illustration by Jan Suermondt.*

When the news reached the bridge that even the escape passages below were afire, Nagumo was advised to transfer his flag to another vessel. The hapless admiral, however, gazed around as if in a trance, unable to comprehend how the fortunes of his proud and mighty fleet had changed so quickly and so brutally in the space of but five minutes. When finally led from the bridge, Nagumo and his staff could only vacate it by sliding down a rope hanging out of one of the windows. Relocating to the *Nagara*, the admiral and his staff contemplated their flame-engulfed flagship as the light cruiser moved away from her at speed. Not until early the following morning did Yamamoto himself give the order for her still burning hulk to be given the *coup de grace*. Dawn was just breaking as four destroyers launched their torpedoes into the mighty ship. She slipped beneath the waves, one last mighty explosion marking her passing as she headed down into the deep, taking with her nearly 300 of her crew.

▲ *With air brakes deployed, the Dauntlesses begin their power-dives from 15,000ft on the Japanese carriers below.* **Akagi, Kaga** *and* **Soryu** *were hit within minutes of each other and were reduced to blazing wrecks by the Navy dive-bombers. (via Robert F. Dorr)*

one of the survivors to a burning hell. As the flames reached the hangar level the stacked bombs blew up, along with the airplanes of the second wave that were still being armed. Within minutes the whole of the lower levels of the carrier were afire and cut off. Just ten minutes after the attack the steering gear failed. Periodically, explosions were felt in the interior of the vessel.

Observers on *Soryu* hardly had time to register the explosions aboard *Kaga* before they, too, became victims of the "Helldivers." Three SBDs plummeted out of the sky just after 1025 to deposit their bombs along her flight deck. Accounts differ as to where the bombs actually hit, but it seems that the first exploded between the second and third lifts. The second hit just in front of the forward lift, penetrated the flight deck, crashed into the hangar level below and exploded amid the aircraft parked there. The subsequent detonation caused the fuel tanks and weapons stores to explode, vaporizing everything within the hangar level and generating a heat

◀ *An SBD of VB-3 recovers aboard the* **Hornet** *having missed the entire battle. A shortage of fuel meant that the whole fighter escort protecting the Dauntlesses had to ditch in the sea. Only the TBDs of* **Hornet's** *Air Group attacked the Japanese carrier fleet. (US Navy)*

so fierce that within a short time even the metal began to melt. Such was the force of this explosion that the forward lift was flung from its mounting and smashed into the island. Simultaneously, the third bomb fell on the rear deck amid the waiting aircraft, transforming it, as on *Kaga* and *Akagi*, into yet another funeral pyre for the élite flyers of the Air Fleet.

Twenty minutes later a huge explosion tore through the innards of the ship, throwing large numbers of men into the water. Such was the destruction and ferocity of the fires aboard *Soryu* that, half an hour after the strike, her engines had stopped, all steering was gone and the whole carrier was ablaze from stem to stern. Seeing that all was lost, her captain gave the order to abandon ship. The destroyers *Hamakaze* and *Isokaze* closed with the blazing hulk and picked up survivors. Attempts to talk Captain Yanagimoto down from the bridge were to no avail, and he was still aboard with sword drawn when, at 1913, a series of massive explosions swept the carrier. She sank shortly afterward, taking 718 men down with her.

## The End of *Yorktown*

Nagumo now devolved command to Rear Admiral Abe Hiraoki in *Tone*, who in turn ordered Yamaguchi and the as yet undamaged *Hiryu* to strike back at the American carriers. At 1058 the first of two strike waves was launched from *Hiryu*, comprising eighteen dive-bombers escorted by six "Zeroes" and led by the redoubtable Lt. Kobayashi. They were guided by radio reports from *Chikuma*'s Number Five floatplane, which had Task Force 17 under discreet surveillance.

Shortly before midday, as *Yorktown* was preparing to recover her dive-bombers and refuel her fighters her radar detected Kobayashi's incoming strike group. A combat air patrol of twelve fighters was already aloft, and a further fifteen were on deck being refueled when the order was given to launch. The dive-bombers were warned off, and the carrier prepared for attack. All her fuel pumps were closed down and the carbonic acid gas fire suppression system was readied. *Yorktown*'s escorts were pulled in closer to add their own firepower to that of the carrier. Fighters were dispatched from Task Force 16, so

that 28 Wildcats were now available to tackle the incoming Japanese aircraft.

Running in at 10,000ft, the "Val" dive-bombers were assailed by the Wildcats and ten, including Kobayashi's, were shot down. The heavy flak curtain sent aloft by the Task Force then accounted for a further three, but five survived. They were sufficient to do the damage. They plummeted down on the *Yorktown*, and three bombs found their mark. The first exploded on the carrier's deck, making a large hole and causing fires which quickly spread below deck. The second crashed down the smokestack and exploded in the engine room, leaving only one boiler working and wrecking the bridge's radar, communications systems and plotting room. The third penetrated the deck and exploded deep in the bowels of the ship, but deft use of the carbonic acid gas system and selective flooding prevented the nearby fuel tanks and a magazine from exploding.

As he was now unable to maintain effective command over the Task Force, Fletcher shifted his flag to the cruiser *Astoria*. However, although *Yorktown* was badly damaged, she was rapidly brought back into action. By 1340 four of her engines were working, the fires were out and she was able to work up 20kts. Rapid deck repairs had been improvised, and she began to recover and refuel her fighters in preparation for *Hiryu*'s second wave.

Meanwhile, the "Judy" reconnaissance aircraft dispatched some hours earlier from the *Soryu* to watch the American force had been recovered aboard *Hiryu*, and Yamaguchi had received the dramatic news that there were three American carriers, not the two suspected. He therefore decided to launch his second strike wave with dispatch. The chosen strike leader was the same Lt. Tomonaga who had led the Midway attack earlier in the day. He accepted without hesitation, even though he knew that his trip would be one way – there had not been enough time to repair the damage to the fuel tank in his port wing. The rapid depletion of Japanese aircraft was apparent in the fact that only sixteen aircraft were available, and even some of these were strays from *Kaga* and *Akagi*. Ten torpedo bombers and six escorting "Zeros" were launched at 1331. Although guided once more by *Chikuma*'s floatplane, Tomonaga's group had been informed that

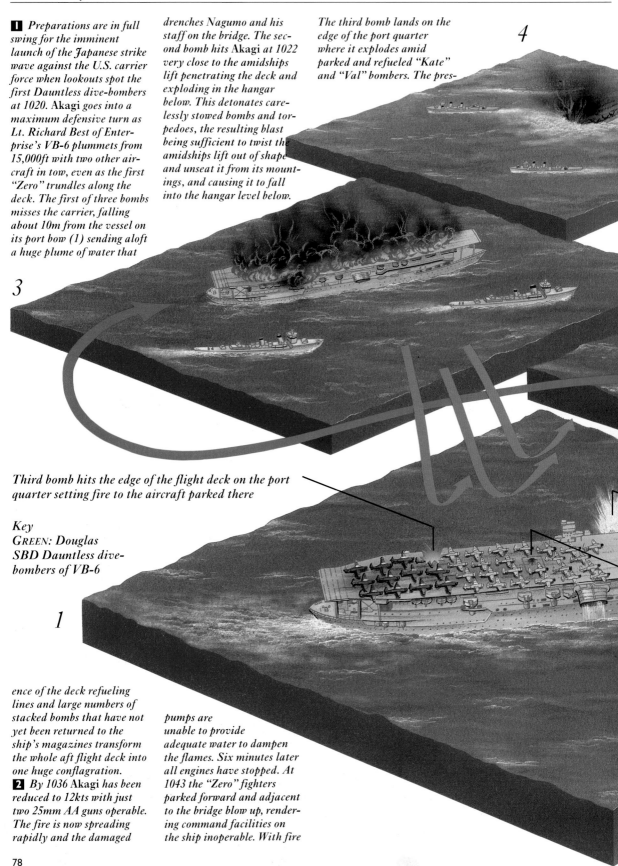

**1** *Preparations are in full swing for the imminent launch of the Japanese strike wave against the U.S. carrier force when lookouts spot the first Dauntless dive-bombers at 1020.* Akagi *goes into a maximum defensive turn as Lt. Richard Best of Enterprise's VB-6 plummets from 15,000ft with two other aircraft in tow, even as the first "Zero" trundles along the deck. The first of three bombs misses the carrier, falling about 10m from the vessel on its port bow (1) sending aloft a huge plume of water that*

*drenches Nagumo and his staff on the bridge. The second bomb hits* Akagi *at 1022 very close to the amidships lift penetrating the deck and exploding in the hangar below. This detonates carelessly stowed bombs and torpedoes, the resulting blast being sufficient to twist the amidships lift out of shape and unseat it from its mountings, and causing it to fall into the hangar level below.*

*The third bomb lands on the edge of the port quarter where it explodes amid parked and refueled "Kate" and "Val" bombers. The pres-*

**4**

**3**

Third bomb hits the edge of the flight deck on the port quarter setting fire to the aircraft parked there

Key
GREEN: Douglas
SBD Dauntless dive-
bombers of VB-6

**1**

*ence of the deck refueling lines and large numbers of stacked bombs that have not yet been returned to the ship's magazines transform the whole aft flight deck into one huge conflagration.*
**2** *By 1036* Akagi *has been reduced to 12kts with just two 25mm AA guns operable. The fire is now spreading rapidly and the damaged*

*pumps are unable to provide adequate water to dampen the flames. Six minutes later all engines have stopped. At 1043 the "Zero" fighters parked forward and adjacent to the bridge blow up, rendering command facilities on the ship inoperable. With fire* in all the passages below and unable to exercise control over his ravaged carrier fleet, Nagumo reluctantly agrees to evacuate the ship, boarding the screening destroyer Nowaki before transferring his command flag to the light cruiser Nagara.

**3** With engine room dead and fires engulfing the ship, Captain Aoki calls up the destroyers Arashi and Nowaki to evacuate all crew not fighting fires. Such is the ferocity of the fires that Aoki and his staff are driven down to the anchor deck where he tries to exercise command over the fire-fighting teams, but to no avail. The Emperor's portrait is transferred at 1338 and shortly thereafter all power from the engines ceases and the blazing hulk begins to drift. Crew evacuation is completed by Arashi and Nowaki by 1600, but it is not until nearly 3½ hrs later that Aoki bows to the inevitable when he signals Nagumo that Akagi cannot be saved and requests permission to scuttle the vessel. By 2000 the two attending destroyers have evacuated the last of the survivors.

**4** Meanwhile Yamamoto, having intercepted Aoki's request to scuttle, orders a delay, no doubt influenced by his own sentimental attachment to the carrier of which once he had been captain. At the same time Aoki returns

Amidships elevator has fallen into the hangar deck below

2

First bomb hits the sea off the port bow approximately 30ft from the carrier

Second bomb hits the amidships elevator at 1022 penetrating and exploding in the hangar below

to Akagi and lashes himself to the ship's anchor, determined to go down with his ship, but he is eventually persuaded to come down and is in due course evacuated by Arashi.

In spite of the terrible damage wrought by the fires and explosions. Akagi stays afloat throughout the night of 4/5 June, but at 0450 Yamamoto reluctantly gives the final order to dispatch the blackened hulk. Shortly after 0450, four destroyers close in on the carrier and launch torpedoes. Just before sunrise, the flagship of the Pearl Harbor Strike Fleet sinks, taking down to the depths some 270 of her crew.

# THE LOSS OF *AKAGI*

**The destruction of the Japanese flagship *Akagi*, 1026 hours to 0500 hours, 4 June 1942**

◄ As the only surviving carrier capable of retaliation, Hiryu launched a strike against Yorktown at 1200. This remarkable photograph was taken literally at the moment of impact when one of three bombs hit the vessel. (via Robert C. Stern)

◄ The following sequence of photographs should be "read" with the diagram on pages 82–3 to give a comprehensive account of the fate of Yorktown. Here she is seen maneuvering to avoid the Japanese bombs while in the next shot she is seen burning after being hit by three bombs from "Val" dive-bombers. (via Robert C. Stern)

▼ Smoke belches forth from the bomb hit that penetrated the stack, extinguishing a large number of her boilers. This damage also led to Fletcher transferring his command flag to the cruiser Astoria. Already, teams can be seen dealing with the damage. (via Robert C. Stern)

▼ Work has already started on repairs to Yorktown's flight deck. Clearly seen is the hole in the splintered flight deck caused by one of the Japanese bombs. Fast work of this sort enabled the carrier to be able to operate her aircraft just in time to receive the second Japanese strike. (via Robert C. Stern)

*Yorktown* had been left ablaze and belching huge columns of smoke, and was presumed to be sinking. So when they arrived in the vicinity of *Yorktown* to discover no evidence of the damage caused by the earlier raid, they assumed that they were about to attack either *Hornet* or *Enterprise*.

Radar had picked up the Japanese group at 1430, and once more the decks of the carrier were rapidly cleared. The twelve Wildcats of the combat air patrol intercepted the incoming force, and as before succeeded in accounting for a number of the attackers, as did antiaircraft fire. Although five bombers and three fighters were lost, the attackers continued to bear in on *Yorktown*. Led by Tomonaga, the five survivors deployed to launch their torpedoes. Having released his own, and knowing he could not

return, the Midway attack leader deliberately crashed his airplane on to *Yorktown*'s flight deck. Two torpedoes then hit the carrier's port side less than 60ft apart, causing a series of explosions and fires. The carrier shuddered under the twin impact and came to a stop, all power was lost and the vessel began to list to port. Fearing that the carrier might capsize, Captain Buckmaster gave the order to abandon ship at 1500 and some 2,270 of her crew were recovered. Although abandoned, she remained afloat and was attended throughout the night by the destroyer *Hughes*, and was still there the following morning. However, the life of this remarkable vessel had not yet run its course. *Yorktown* refused to sink and was still afloat early the next morning, and her captain believed it was still possible to salvage her.

▶ **Yorktown** *is seen here shortly after 1220 by which time she was dead in the water. Most of the fires however have been contained, although a small amount of smoke is still emerging from the stack. (via Robert C. Stern)*

▶ *By 1437,* **Yorktown,** *able to make speed once again, prepares to launch eight of the ten fighters left on board against the incoming second Japanese strike. (via Robert C. Stern)*

▶ *Although a grainy photograph, this picture captures the second strike on the* **Yorktown** *which was carried out only by "Kate" torpedo bombers. Nevertheless, such had been the success of the U.S. repair teams that Japanese flyers believed*

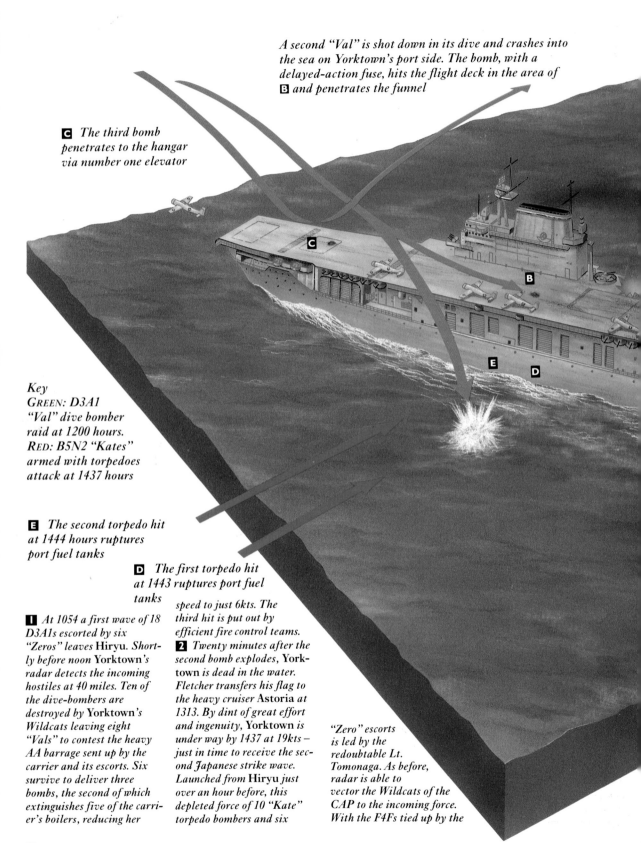

A second "Val" is shot down in its dive and crashes into the sea on Yorktown's port side. The bomb, with a delayed-action fuse, hits the flight deck in the area of **B** and penetrates the funnel

**C** The third bomb penetrates to the hangar via number one elevator

Key
GREEN: D3A1 "Val" dive bomber raid at 1200 hours. RED: B5N2 "Kates" armed with torpedoes attack at 1437 hours

**E** The second torpedo hit at 1444 hours ruptures port fuel tanks

**D** The first torpedo hit at 1443 ruptures port fuel tanks

**1** At 1054 a first wave of 18 D3A1s escorted by six "Zeros" leaves Hiryu. Shortly before noon Yorktown's radar detects the incoming hostiles at 40 miles. Ten of the dive-bombers are destroyed by Yorktown's Wildcats leaving eight "Vals" to contest the heavy AA barrage sent up by the carrier and its escorts. Six survive to deliver three bombs, the second of which extinguishes five of the carrier's boilers, reducing her speed to just 6kts. The third hit is put out by efficient fire control teams.

**2** Twenty minutes after the second bomb explodes, Yorktown is dead in the water. Fletcher transfers his flag to the heavy cruiser Astoria at 1313. By dint of great effort and ingenuity, Yorktown is under way by 1437 at 19kts – just in time to receive the second Japanese strike wave. Launched from Hiryu just over an hour before, this depleted force of 10 "Kate" torpedo bombers and six

"Zero" escorts is led by the redoubtable Lt. Tomonaga. As before, radar is able to vector the Wildcats of the CAP to the incoming force. With the F4Fs tied up by the

# THE LOSS OF *YORKTOWN*

## The saga of *Yorktown*, 1050 hours on 4 June to 0500 hours on 7 June 1942

Approaching on a curving path, the first "Val" dives but disintegrates under Yorktown's AA fire and falls into the sea in three pieces, but the bomb hits the flight deck and explodes **A**

"Zeros," the surviving "Kates" speed in on Task Force 17 at low level. Although five are hacked down by the "splash barrage," four break through to launch their torpedoes. Having successfully avoided two of these by deft maneuvering Yorktown succumbs to two strikes. The consequences are dramatic: her port fuel tanks

are destroyed and her rudder jammed: almost immediately she begins to take on a 26° list to port.
**3** Unable to maintain watertight integrity, the carrier is in danger of capsizing, so at about 1500 Captain Buckmaster orders the vessel abandoned. Four destroyers, Balch, Benham, Russell and Anderson close with Yorktown saving some 2,270 of her crew. She is now abandoned, Fletcher and Buckmaster presuming her list is such that it is only a matter of time before she sinks.

When Yorktown detects the incoming second strike, at approximately 1320, only 10 Wildcats are on board. Only 8 possess enough fuel for combat and are launched immediately to intercept the torpedo bombers, along with 6 F4Fs of VF-3 that are already on patrol

**4** But the following morning Yorktown is still afloat. The decision is taken to reboard her, and a determined effort is made to salvage the stricken carrier.

Nimitz dispatches the minesweeper Vireo and fleet tug Navajo to assist and also strengthens the antisubmarine screen around the ship. At 1436 Vireo begins to tow Yorktown toward Pearl Harbor at 2kts, while aboard the carrier the salvage team lightens the vessel by ejecting over the side extraneous materials until nightfall when the vessel is without

power and illumination.
**5** At 0410 in the early light of 6 June the Japanese submarine I-168 sights Yorktown screened by six destroyers: not until 1331 can torpedoes be fired. The first hits the destroyer Hamman which sinks almost immediately; two torpedoes run under the destroyer's keep and slam into the York-

town's vitals, but still the carrier refuses to die.
**6** Ironically, the water pouring into Yorktown's starboard side now levels up the list, and Buckmaster is optimistic. The carrier hangs on through the night but it becomes ever clearer that she is doomed. USS Yorktown sinks as the sun rises, at 0458 on 7 June.

◀ *Attempts to salvage* Yorktown *and tow her to Pearl Harbor were finally abandoned on 6 June when she was torpedoed by the Japanese submarine* I-168. *Hit by two "fish," it rapidly became clear that she was beyond saving. In the two center photographs she is seen having taken on a heavy list to port while still surrounded by her destroyer screen. Bottom: With the ever-increasing list, salvage teams are ordered to abandon ship and they can be seen moving down the starboard hull to be picked up by an attendant destroyer. The cross on the hull marks the likely position of a torpedo hit from* I-168. *(via Robert C. Stern)*

By midday on 5 June a salvage team had been put aboard, and considerable progress was being made when disaster struck. Earlier that morning *Yorktown* had been spotted by one of *Chikuma*'s floatplanes, and Yamamoto had ordered the submarine *I-168*, standing to off Midway Island, where she had carried out a night bombardment in the early hours of 5 June, to "locate and destroy the American carrier." Shortly after 1300 on 6 June the submarine penetrated the five-destroyer screen around the carrier and fired a spread of four torpedoes. The destroyer *Hamman*, which was lashed to the carrier, was cut in two by a torpedo and sank at once. Tragically, her rapid descent set off her depth charges, killing many of her crew who were in the water. Two torpedoes slammed into *Yorktown*, causing damage that Buckmaster knew put the carrier beyond any hope of salvage. Nevertheless, the obstinate carrier did not finally succumb until 0600 the following morning.

Just as the survivors of *Hiryu*'s strike force returned to the carrier, she was finally spotted by one of the ten scout aircraft Fletcher had dispatched earlier to seek her out. Lieutenant Wallace Short found her and her screening vessels approximately

100 miles to the northwest of *Yorktown*. When the news was received by Spruance aboard *Enterprise*, the decision was taken to launch an all-out strike against *Hiryu*. At 1530 *Enterprise* dispatched a force of 24 Dauntlesses, and *Hornet* launched another sixteen. The few Wildcats that had survived the day's combat were retained to defend the carriers, so the dive-bombers made way toward their prey without fighter cover.

By 1630 the remnant of the second strike group had been recovered by the *Hiryu*. Only three "Zeros" and five "Kates" had returned, but the pilots of the torpedo bombers were convinced that, rather than attacking *Yorktown* again, they had successfully destroyed a second U.S. carrier. Yamaguchi now believed that, with the odds reduced to one-to-one, it might still be possible to resurrect a possible victory out of the ashes of the morning's disaster. To that end he ordered a third air strike made ready. However, the aircraft available were but a pale shadow of *Hiryu*'s air group and of the First Air Fleet's airplane strength launched against Midway barely twelve hours before. Only four "Kates," five "Vals" and six "Zeros" of the combat air patrol, along with their exhausted crews, could be mustered. Nevertheless, the order went out to refuel and rearm them for a twilight strike. The deck of *Hiryu* rapidly became a hive of activity as fuel lines, bombs, torpedoes and ammunition were deployed to arm and equip the skeleton strike force. In the meantime, the aircrew were treated to a meal of sweet rice balls before their anticipated launch at 1800. While the Japanese flyers were in the middle of their meal the first Dauntlesses began their dive on the last of Nagumo's carriers.

## The Death of *Hiryu*

Although there was a small combat air patrol aloft, the "Zeros" did not detect the incoming dive-bombers, so when the first thirteen of the SBDs began their power dives they achieved complete surprise. They came out of the sun, as they had done against the other carriers earlier in the day, allowing the *Hiryu* and its screening vessels to put up only a desultory defensive barrage before the first bombs struck. Sharp commands from the bridge to the engine room saw the speed of the *Hiryu* race up to 30kts as the rudder was put hard to starboard. From the diving SBDs it could be seen that she was attempting to turn full circle, but it was to no avail. Although three bombs were avoided. Nemesis struck with number four and three others followed in rapid succession. Two hit amidships and the other two forward of the island. The first blew the forward lift against the island bridge, and the whole deck forward of that position became a vast flaming void. As before, bombs penetrated to the hangar levels, causing casually stashed bombs to explode and fuel tanks to erupt. Many dead lay on the flight deck, and large numbers of the crew who survived the initial explosions below succumbed to the thick smoke from oil fires. The small strike group spotted on the rear of the carrier also blew up, spewing flaming fuel across the deck and adding further misery to the suffering crew.

Judging that *Hiryu* was already fatally damaged, the other SBDs turned their attention to the vessels of the screening force. *Haruna*, *Tone* and *Chikuma* were all subjected to heavy attack, but none were hit. With the departure of the American airplanes attempts were made to control the fires raging on the carrier. However, such was the damage that all the fire-fighting equipment had been destroyed, and the surviving crewmen were reduced to using buckets on lines and seawater in a pathetic attempt to control the flames. Four destroyers pulled alongside and poured seawater from their hoses onto the flaming hull. It was to no avail. Having maintained speed for some while after the attack, the engines finally died when flames reached the lower levels, killing many of the engineering crew. Heat caused rupturing of the lower hull plates, which led to flooding, and as she took on water *Hiryu* developed a fifteen-degree list.

A large explosion at 0158, which caused the fires to increase in intensity, finally decided Admiral Yamaguchi to abandon ship. When ordered to muster at 0250, approximately half of the crew of 1,500 had survived to present themselves. While the officers and crew were transferred to the destroyers alongside, Admiral Yamaguchi and Captain Kaku stayed aboard the stricken vessel, having stated their intention of going down with her. Lashing themselves to the helm, they awaited the end. On the order of Captain Abe, the destroyer *Makigumo*

launched a spread of torpedoes at the flaming hulk, and it was assumed that in the wake of the subsequent explosions the carrier would inevitably sink. But, like the *Yorktown*, the *Hiryu* did not want to die. She did not finally founder until about 0820, carrying with her to the bottom 416 of her crew, her captain and Admiral Yamaguchi. The last carrier of Nagumo's victorious and proud First Air Fleet had been consigned to the depths.

### Operation MI Canceled

Although Yamamoto and his staff had been party to the messages dispatched by the *Tone*'s floatplane throughout the morning, the only signal they received from Nagumo came shortly after 0835. It announced the sighting of a carrier and other vessels, its position, and the decision to head for it. Although the operational plan had made no allowance for this contingency, Yamamoto and his staff displayed no anxiety, remaining secure in the conviction that Nagumo could handle the situation and resolve it to their advantage. The shock at the

▲ *Caught by the SBDs, the* Hiryu *tried desperately to avoid the plummeting dive-bombers but to no avail. At 1705* *she was bracketed by four bombs and her fate became very quickly that of her sister carriers. (U.S. National Archives)*

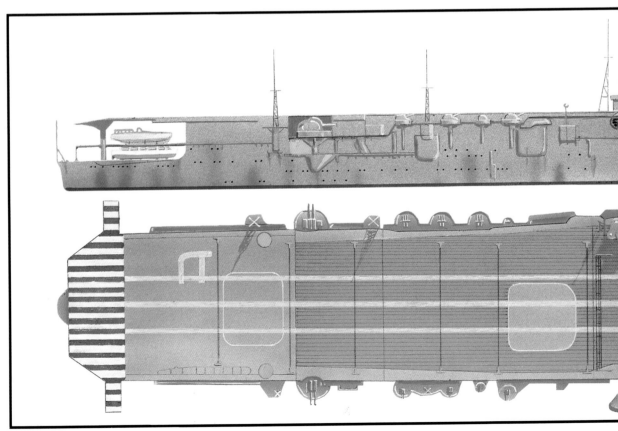

▲ Hiryu *is seen here dead in the water. A tremendous explosion has flipped her forward lift through the air to rest against the vessel's island structure.*

*The whole of the flight deck just forward of the island is a gaping void and the hangar level below can be clearly seen. (U.S. National Archives)*

receipt of Admiral Abe's 1050 signal announcing: "Fires raging aboard *Kaga*, *Soryu* and *Akagi* resulting from attacks by enemy carrier and land based planes" was therefore profound and traumatic. Reputedly, Yamamoto's response was to emit a deep groan, and the mood of his staff moved rapidly from bright optimism to deep despair. The only saving grace was that Abe reported *Hiryu* untouched and fighting back.

Pondering his options in the wake of these dire tidings, Yamamoto decided on a course of action that he believed still offered the Japanese the chance to retrieve the situation. At 1220 he issued a signal ordering a concentration of Kondo's Second Fleet with his own Main Body to the northwest of Midway at 1200 the following day. AL was suspended, and Kakuta was ordered to send his two carriers southward posthaste to effect a junction with Yamamoto, but it soon became apparent that *Ryujo* and *Junyo* could not arrive before the afternoon of 6 June. At this stage Yamamoto still believed he could overwhelm the enemy by sheer weight of numbers in a night battle.

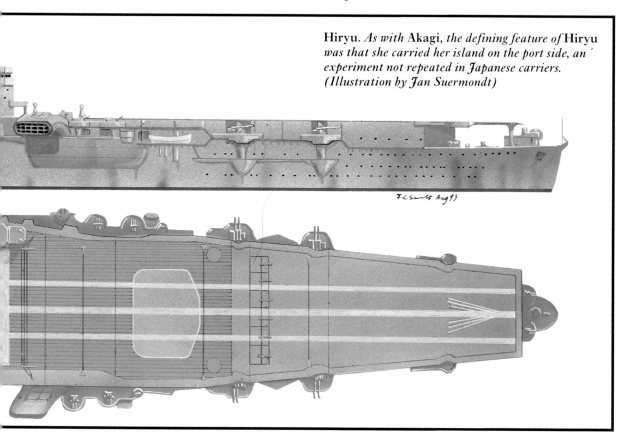

**Hiryu.** *As with* **Akagi,** *the defining feature of* **Hiryu** *was that she carried her island on the port side, an experiment not repeated in Japanese carriers. (Illustration by Jan Suermondt)*

Subsequently, Kondo was further ordered to detach Kurita's four heavy cruisers from his Main Body and send them toward Midway to continue a night bombardment to be initiated by submarine *I-168* shortly after midnight on 5 June. As the day wore on, however, the news feeding back to Yamamoto became increasingly serious. Shortly after 1700 he knew that he had also lost *Hiryu*, the linchpin of his updated plan. Although intelligence on the size of the American force was confusing, it was now known to contain at least three carriers. By 1915, as he received word of Spruance's withdrawal of Task Force 16 to the east, he knew his chances of catching them in a night battle were rapidly receding. At 2130 Nagumo signaled that he was in essence unable to cooperate with the Main Body in any night attack. Adjudging him to be too "conservative," Yamamoto replaced Nagumo with Kondo at 0055.

As the hours wore on it became increasingly clear that the American force was moving away from the Japanese at too fast a rate to allow them to be caught in a night engagement. Furthermore, Kurita's cruisers could not begin their bombardment of Midway before 0300. They and Kondo's battleships would then be exposed to air attack, not just from Midway, but also from the U.S. carriers that were expected to make another appearance with the onset of daylight at 0400. So it was that, with great reluctance, Yamamoto had the signal flashed to all vessels canceling Operation MI and ordering a general withdrawal at 0255 on 5 June. Kondo's main force linked up with the Main Body at about 0700 when they were some 320 miles northwest of Midway, to be joined at midday by the remnants of Nagumo's once proud and mighty First Air Fleet. But as the still-powerful Japanese fleet turned west and headed for home, the agony of the Combined Fleet had not yet run its course.

## 5 June: The Demise of *Mikuma* and *Mogami*

Far to the southwest of Yamamoto's Main Body, Kurita's Cruiser Division 7 was but 80 miles from Midway when calamity struck early on 5 June. The four cruisers were in single column when, at about 0118, the sighting of a U.S. submarine led Kurita to order an emergency 45-degree turn. As a conse-

quence of confusion *Mogami* rammed *Mikuma* on her port quarter. Damage to both vessels was severe, with *Mogami*'s bow bent back right to her No. 1 turret and *Mikuma*'s port side oil tanks holed. Leaving the destroyers *Asashio* and *Arashio* to escort the two cruisers, Kurita headed off to rendezvous with Yamamoto. Although *Mogami* was still able to make 12kts, *Mikuma* was leaving a wide oil slick in her wake, and this telltale trail allowed a PBY to locate the four vessels shortly after 0630. Between 0805 and 0828 the cruisers were attacked by Dauntlesses, Vindicators and B-17s from Midway. There were no bomb hits, but one Vindicator hit by antiaircraft fire crashed onto the aft turret of the *Mikuma*, and the ensuing fire spread down into the engine compartment. *Mikuma*'s speed was now reduced to that of *Mogami*.

The following day *Hornet* and *Enterprise* both launched strikes against the two cruisers. In three attacks through to 1445 *Mogami* was extensively damaged by at least six bomb hits from SBDs, but was able to limp back to Truk by 14 June. However, her sister ship was so extensively damaged in the attacks that her captain ordered her abandoned even before the third strike. She was afire from stem to stern, and *Arashio* had great difficulty closing to rescue survivors because of the intensity of the heat. A further bomb hit by the last SBD strike set off her torpedoes, and she was abandoned and sank after sunset on 6 June. Nearly 300 crewmen were killed, and her demise marked the end of the Battle of Midway.

# THE AFTERMATH

There can be little doubt that, with the news of the destruction of the *Hiryu*, Admiral Yamamoto knew that more than just the battle had been lost. Midway marked the moment when Japan lost the war, and was for that reason the decisive battle of the Pacific conflict. The four carriers of Nagumo's First Air Fleet had been Japan's primary offensive instrument in her bid for hegemony in the Pacific. With their destruction, Japan's superiority in naval air power – the key to the successful execution of offensive warfare in the vast Pacific theater – was eliminated. In one fell swoop Nimitz had wrested the offensive initiative from Japan, and thereafter the United States was never to surrender it. Whereas before Midway Japanese naval strategy had been predicated upon *shinko sakusen*, or offensive operations, thereafter all was perceived in terms of *yogeki sakusen* – defensive operations.

The reality of the catastrophic defeat at Midway was the elimination of irreplaceable assets from the Japanese order of battle. Above all, there were the experienced pilots now lost forever as a consequence of the totally inadequate pilot replacement program with which Japan had entered the war.

Nor could Japanese shipyards hope to replace the four lost fleet carriers. At the time of the outbreak of the Pacific conflict, Japanese shipyards had yet to adopt the mass-production shipbuilding techniques practiced so successfully in the United States. An indication of the production differential between American and Japanese yards in the construction of aircraft carriers can be gauged by a comparison of the production figures for this class of warship in the two and a half years from Pearl Harbor through to June 1944.

The United States completed 18 of the formidable Essex-class fleet carriers and 99 escort carriers, whereas Japan produced just twelve carriers of all types. Furthermore, this superiority was not just numerical but also qualitative, the U.S. vessels being better built and fitted out with superior technical equipment. This was already discernible at the time of Midway. Nearly all U.S. vessels in the battle were provided with radar, whereas in the Combined Fleet this vital equipment had been fitted in an experimental capacity only to the battleships *Ise* and *Hyuga*, which were engaged in the Aleutians sideshow and were therefore put to no good use. In the months and years following Midway, the relentless destruction of the once proud and mighty Combined Fleet by the most powerful navy the world has yet seen completely shattered

◀ *For the Rengo Kantai, the agony of Midway did not end with the loss of the carriers. Due to a collision, the heavy cruiser* **Mikuma** *of Admiral Kurita's unfortunately named Midway Bombardment Force was heavily damaged in a collision* *with her sister ship* **Mogami** *in the early hours of 5 June. Throughout the day both vessels were subjected to heavy air attacks. This is* **Mikuma** *having been hit by SBDs from USS* **Enterprise.** *(U.S. National Archives)*

the fallacious notion of the primacy of *Nihon Seishin* over the material and technological superiority of the United States.

The American victory at Midway was a remarkable testimony to the bravery, self-sacrifice, foresight and technical expertise of the U.S. Navy. Indeed, Professor Samuel Morison emphasized the latter point when he spoke of Midway as "a victory of intelligence." The breaking of the Japanese code JN-25 provided Nimitz with a remarkable oversight of his enemy's intentions, but a very great deal could have gone awry between planning and victory. Nor was the American performance in the battle flawless. In the final analysis, however, those errors were far fewer and less profound by degrees of magnitude than those of the Japanese.

What if Midway had indeed proved to be Yamamoto's *kantai kessen*? It is almost certain that he would have been profoundly disappointed in his expectations of the benefits that he hoped Japan would gain from victory. In this sense it would have transpired that victory was anything but "decisive." Any material damage the Japanese might have inflicted on the Pacific Fleet could never have been enough to bring the United States to the peace table. Indeed, this could have been the only tangible consequence that would have shown Midway to have been the "decisive" battle for Japan. In this, his hopes for the results of a Midway "victory" would have been totally forlorn. Indeed, it could be argued that the very fact that Yamamoto entertained such hopes was evidence of a profound mis-

understanding of the psychology of the nation he professed to know so well.

Yamamoto's failure to perceive that no lasting political benefit could accrue to Japan from what would have been a purely military victory at Midway is symptomatic of the intellectual failure that lay at the heart of the Combined Fleet's warmaking strategy. In seeing "victory" purely in terms of territory and resources captured and battles won, the Japanese had truly misunderstood the nature of the war they had unleashed. Yamamoto had cast the die for the nature of the Pacific conflict with his attack on Pearl Harbor. The images of the devastated warships and the dead personnel created by his flyers on 7 December 1941 had succeeded in unifying the politically disparate American people in a way no domestic politician had ever done, filling them with a bitter resolve to see the perpetrators of that attack utterly and totally defeated, no matter what the cost. That, indeed, was the point. Japan had unwittingly initiated a "total war" with a power that not only possessed the resources and expertise to prosecute such a war, but was above all else animated by the moral conviction and certitude to harness and direct its national resources to serve such a conflict and see it through to its bitter end. Had the Japanese triumphed at Midway, it certainly would have taken the United States longer to achieve the same end they realized in August 1945. The cost in blood and treasure would have been far higher, but the result would have been the same – the inevitable and total ruin of the Japanese Empire.

◄ Mikuma *some hours before her demise: on top of her 8in turret No. 4 can be seen the remains of a Marine Vindicator dive-bomber. Hanging out over the side of the vessel are her torpedo tubes.* Mikuma *finally sank after sunset on 6 June. (U.S. National Archives)*

# CHRONOLOGY

Note: Japanese dates are given in Japanese time until 3 June, after which the time used is local; i.e., Japanese time for N-Day = 7 June, by local time becomes 6 June. All dates and times in parentheses are approximate.

**1941**

**7 Dec** Japanese attack Pearl Harbor.

**31 Dec** Admiral Chester Nimitz assumes command of the Pacific Fleet.

**1942**

**1–14 Jan** Admiral Ugaki, on instructions from Yamamoto, prepares plans identifying possible future operations.

**20–25 Feb** Army turns down Navy project to invade Ceylon.

**Mid March** Combined Fleet turns to Midway proposal.

**28 March** Combined Fleet staff under Kuroshima begin work on Midway operation.

**2–5 April** Kuroshima and Watanabe discuss Midway plan with Naval General Staff. They reluctantly agree to accept Midway plan after Yamamoto threatens to resign.

**18 April** Doolittle raid.

**22 April** First Air Fleet returns to Japan. Nagumo learns of Midway operation for first time.

**28 & 29 April** Conference aboard *Yamato* to explore Midway operation.

**1–4 May** Preliminary war games for MI held on *Yamato*.

**2 May** Nimitz flies to Midway to inspect defenses of base.

**5 May** Admiral Nagano issues Naval Order 18, ordering MI and AL.

**7-11 May** Battle of Coral Sea. U.S. loses *Lexington*. *Yorktown* badly damaged. Japan loses *Shoho*. *Shokaku* and *Zuikaku* unavailable to take part in MI because of battle damage/airplane losses.

**10 May** Midway dispatches false message under Hypo's direction that Midway is short of water.

**12 May** Hypo intercepts Japanese signal that "AF" is short of water.

**15 May** Halsey ordered to Pearl Harbor.

**20 May** Yamamoto issues estimate of U.S. strength.

**20 May** Midway Transport Group & Seaplane Tender Group leave Japan for Saipan.

**21 May** Midway begins Alert Phase.

**22 May** Midway begins search and reconnaissance phase.

**24 May** Final wargames on *Yamato*.

**25 May** Commander Rochefort gives Nimitz breakdown of Japanese order of battle.

**25 May** Nimitz informs Midway that D-Day is postponed to 3 June.

**22–26 May** Air and Marine reinforcements arrive at Midway.

**26 May** Halsey too ill to command TF 16. Recommends Spruance.

**27 May** First Carrier Strike Force sorties from Japan. Midway Invasion Force and Seaplane Tender Group sorties from Saipan. Close Support Group sorties from Guam.

**27 May** Nimitz briefs Spruance. *Yorktown* enters harbor. Emergency repair work begins.

**28 May** Northern Force sorties from Japan.

**28 May** Fletcher named commander of Task Forces 16 & 17. Nimitz briefs Fletcher and Spruance. Task Force 16 sorties from Pearl Harbor.

**29 May** Yamamoto's Main Body sorties from Hasharijima.

**30 May** Submarine finds U.S. vessels at French Frigate Shoals. Operation K postponed.

**30 May** Task Force 17 sorties from Pearl.

**30 May** Midway begins air search. Time uncertain: Japanese submarine cordon arrives on station 2 days late. Does not detect passage of either U.S. Task Force.

**31 May** Operation K canceled.

**1 June** Japanese detect U.S. vessels sending many "urgent" messages.

**2 June** Nagumo breaks radio silence by transmitting course change.

**2 June** TF 16 & TF 17 meet at "Point Luck."

**3 June:**

**0300** Second Carrier Strike Force launches air strike.

**0800-0808** Attacks Dutch Harbor.

**0904** PBY 6-V-55 sights Japanese vessels.

**0925** Ensign Reid sends message "Sighted Main Body." Time uncertain: Tanaka informs Yamamoto Invasion Force sighted.

**1125** Read sends report listing 11 vessels sighted.

**1200** 2nd Carrier Strike Force withdraws toward Adak.

**1225** Sweeney leads 9 B-17s to hit Invasion Force.

**1640** Invasion Force bombed by B-17s. No hits.

**1950** Fletcher orders TF 16 & 17 south.

**2115** 4 PBYs leave Midway to attack Invasion Force.

**4 June:**

**0130** 3 PBYs attack Invasion Force. *Akebono Maru* hit.

**0245** Aircrew awoken on Japanese carriers.

**0300** Reveille on Midway.

**0400** Midway launches PBYs followed by B-17s.

**0430** 108 airplanes of First Strike Wave launched. *Akagi*, *Kaga* and *Haruna* launch scout aircraft.

**0430** *Yorktown* launches ten scout SBDs.

**0438** *Chikuma* launches No. 5 floatplane.

**0437** Dawn.

**0438** *Chikuma* launches No. 6 floatplane.

**0442** *Tone* launches No. 3 floatplane.

**0500** *Tone* launches No. 4 floatplane.

**0530** Ensign Ady reports a carrier.

**0534** *Enterprise* receives same report.

**0553** Midway radar picks up Strike Wave.

**0556** Fighters take off from Midway. Air Raid alert sounded.

**0600** Sweeney's B-17s diverted to attack carriers.

**0603** Spruance receives news of two enemy carriers.

**0607** Fletcher orders Spruance to move toward carriers and launch attack.

**0610** VMSB airplanes take off from Midway.

**0615** VT-8 TBFs take off from Midway.

**0616** Midway fighters attack Japanese strike group.

**0630-0643** Japanese strike on Midway.

**0700** *Hornet* launches airplanes.

**0705** Tomonaga radios "need for second strike on Midway."

**0706** *Enterprise* launches her strike group.

**0702-0830** Successive waves of Midway-based aircraft attack First Air Fleet. Heavy U.S. losses, no Japanese carriers hit.

**0715** Nagumo orders second wave "Kate" re-equipped with bombs.

**0728** *Tone*'s No. 4 airplane signals what appears to be ten enemy surface ships.

**0745** Nagumo orders torpedoes still on "Kates" to be left on.

**0800** *Tone* No. 4 airplane ordered to "ascertain ship types."

**0806** Reports back "enemy fleet consists of five cruisers and five destroyers."

**0830** No. 4 airplane now reports enemy ships include "what appears to be a carrier."

**0837** Tomonaga's aircraft begin recovery aboard carriers.

**0838** *Yorktown* begins launch of airplanes.

**0845** More scout aircraft launched to ascertain more details of U.S. vessels.

**0855** Nagumo orders carrier force northward once Midway airplanes recovered.

**0917** Fleet turns on new heading ENE to close with U.S. carrier.

**0918** All aircraft recovered by Japanese carriers.

**0918** *Chikuma* sights VT-8.

**0920** VT-8 attacks.

**0955** McClusky sights wake of Japanese destroyer.

**0958** VT-6 attacks Carrier Fleet.

**1005** McClusky sights Japanese fleet. Leslie does same.

**1015-1020** VT-3 begins attack on First Air Fleet.

**1020** SBDs sighted over Fleet. *Akagi* goes into maximum turn.

**1022** *Kaga* dive-bombed.

**1024** Extensive fires break out on *Kaga*.

**1025** *Soryu* bombed three times.

**1026** *Akagi* hit by two bombs.

**1046** Nagumo and staff abandon *Akagi* for *Nagara*.

**1050** Nagumo informs Yamamoto of fate of three carriers.

**1055** Crew aboard *Soryu* ordered to abandon ship.

**1058** *Hiryu* launches first strike wave.

**1127** *Akagi* stopped.

**1200** *Hiryu* attacks *Yorktown*.

**1220** Yamamoto orders concentration of Main Body, Invasion Force and 2nd Mobile Carrier Force.

**1310** Yamamoto temporarily suspends MI and AL.

**1320** *Hiryu* launches second strike.

**1437** *Yorktown* still making 19kts.

**1445** *Hiryu* located. Spruance orders immediate attack.

**1454** *Hiryu* reports two definite hits on *Yorktown*, although Japanese believe it to be a second carrier.

**1455** Abandon ship ordered on *Yorktown*.

**1550** All aircraft launched from *Hornet* and *Enterprise*.

**1640** Captain Amagai orders abandon ship on *Kaga*.

**1705** *Hiryu* attacked, hit by four bombs.

**1913** *Soryu* sinks.

**1925** *Kaga* sinks.

**2000** All hands abandon *Akagi*.

**5 June:**

**0130** Submarine *I-168* bombards Midway.

**0200** Spruance turns west.

**0255** Yamamoto cancels MI.

**0300** *Mikuma* crashes into *Mogami*.

**0500** *Akagi* scuttled.

**0820** *Hiryu* sinks.

**0840** First air attack on Japanese cruisers.

**6 June:**

**0945-1445** Air attacks on *Mikuma* and *Mogami*.

**1331** *I-168* torpedoes *Yorktown*.

After sunset *Mikuma* sinks. *Mogami* limps back to Truk.

**7 June** *Yorktown* sinks at 0458.

# A GUIDE TO FURTHER READING

AGAWA, H. *The Reluctant Admiral*, Kodansha International Ltd., 1979.

CALVOCORESSI, P., WINT, G. and PRITCHARD, J. *Total War: The Causes and Courses of the Second World War*, Vol II, Penguin Books, 1989.

DULL, P. S. *A Battle History of the Imperial Japanese Navy*, U.S. Naval Institute Press, 1978.

FUCHIDA, M. and OKUMIYA, M. *Midway*, U.S. Naval Institute Press, 1955, reprinted 1992.

HOWARTH, S. *Morning Glory*, Hamish Hamilton, 1983.

IENAGA, S. *The Pacific War, 1931–1945*, Pantheon Books, 1968.

OKUMIYA, M., HORIKOSHI, J. *Zero*, Cassell, 1957.

PRANGE, G. *At Dawn We Slept*, McGraw Hill, 1981.

— *Miracle At Midway*, McGraw Hill, 1982.

UGAKI, M. (ed. D. M. Goldstein and K. V. Dillon) *Fading Victory: The Diary of Admiral Ugaki*, University of Pittsburgh Press, 1991.

VAN DER VAT, D. *The Pacific Campaign*, Hodder & Stoughton, 1991.

WILMOT, H. P. *Empires in the Balance*, U.S. Naval Institute Press, 1982.

General Reference:

KEEGAN, J. (ed.) *The Times Atlas of the Second World War*, Times Books, 1989.

PITT, B. *Purnell's History of the Second World War*, Macdonald Phoebus/BPC Publishing Ltd., 1966.

# WARGAMING MIDWAY

How does one go about wargaming a real-life operation that was tested out as a wargame by one of the actual participants? This is one of the problems which faces any wargamer who wants to refight the Battle of Midway. Another is the sheer size of the operation, in terms of both the geographical area covered and the number of ships and aircraft involved. It would be possible, with enough players and enough room, to go through each phase of the prebattle preparations and the battle itself, and recreate the whole thing, but this is a luxury unknown outside of the military and a few very large wargames groups which have expertise in running megagames. For the majority of wargamers, who may perhaps only have sessions of between three and five hours in which to fight their wargames, a more practical solution is to split the whole operation up into a series of related and interlocking wargames.

A prime example of this approach was the series of games about the German World War One cruiser SMS *Königsberg*, which were created by Tim Price and published in *Wargames Illustrated* (Nos. 60 to 63), and entitled "The Germans Who Never Lost." The games included a strategic map game, a naval gunnery game, and a tabletop tactical game. These games were designed so that they could be played as separate "stand-alone" games, or they could be integrated to form one large game, depending upon the time available and the individual preferences of the wargamers. Such an approach would be an excellent way in which to wargame the Battle of Midway. The whole operation could be split down into a series of strategic and tactical games, each of which would be able to "stand-alone" and yet also lead on to the next game.

The most obvious starting point for the strategic level games would be a committee game which dealt with the decision making process of the Imperial General Headquarters, and its relationships with the Imperial Japanese Army and the Imperial Japanese Navy. A similar game could be set up to deal with the conflicting views about the future strategy to be adopted by the U.S. and her allies in the Pacific. In the latter case the role of intelligence gathering would be of major importance, and this could be dealt with by making one of the game umpires a "plumpire" (player/umpire) who could feed the relevant information into the game at the appropriate moment.

Games of this type have gained much wider acceptance among wargamers in recent years, thanks mainly to the work done by Dr. Paddy Griffith, and the techniques involved are fairly well known. In this case players could be given briefings and personal goals based upon the information contained in the relevant chapter in this book, and would be expected to try to achieve their goals whilst also producing a workable strategic plan.

The Matrix Game is a somewhat newer concept than the committee game, although they do share several similar features, i.e., each player has a personal briefing and agenda for success. It was first developed in the U.S. by Chris Engle, and since then it has matured into a very simple yet sophisticated method of dealing with the political, planning, and strategic aspects of a campaign. During each move the players have to put forward one "argument" (which comprises an "Action," a "Result," and up to three "Reasons") as to what would happen next in the campaign. Once all the "arguments" for one move have been presented, they are then adjudicated upon by the umpire, and their success (or otherwise) depends upon the strength of the "argument."

The matrix game has the major advantages over the committee game of being quick to learn, fast to play, and generally requiring fewer players and only one umpire. It has the further advantage of producing a very narrative style of game, which many players find very easy to follow. Further information about this style of gaming can be found in the pages of *The Experimental Games Group Newsletter* (published by Chris Engle in the U.S.), *The Nugget Games Group Newsletter* (published by Wargame Developments in the U.K.), and *Wargames Illustrated*.

Once the basic strategy has been devised by the committee game or the matrix game, the players can move on to the map game. This would entail the use of a large map of the Pacific area, upon which are marked the major bases in use by both sides at the time of the battle. The map could be a modern map purchased from one of the larger stationers or High Street booksellers, a hand drawn copy or photocopied enlargement of a map from one of the numerous histories of the Second World War, the Pacific Campaign or this particular battle, or a map from one of the several board games which deal with the Battle for Midway. The important thing is that the map must have the relevant information on it and be large enough to allow the positions of the forces involved to be marked easily.

The difficulty with map games is ensuring that an accurate plot of the positions of the opposing forces is maintained as they move about the ocean and (hopefully) into contact. It must be remembered that ships and aircraft do not move at full speed all the time, and that this must be taken into account, as should the problems of refueling. F. T. Jane (of *Fighting Ships* fame) came up with a very simple and accurate method for doing this at the beginning of the 20th Century, and one can do no better than to adopt his system. Further information can be obtained by buying or reading a copy of his *How to Play the "Naval War Game"* (published in 1912, and republished in 1990 by Bill Leeson).

Tactical-level games come to the fore once both sides have come into contact with one another. There are numerous tactical-level games which can be used to fight out the actual battle, but the main problem to be dealt with is the distances between the forces when the battle actually begins. It might just be possible to set up both sides on one playing surface, but the size of the room required would be prohibitive unless one was using very small-scale ships (at 1:3000 scale a scale distance of 100 nautical miles is 200 feet!) and one was prepared to distort the scales involved.

The solution to this problem lies in the fact that neither side comes within heavy gun range of the other during the Battle of Midway, and so there is no need to set the whole thing up in a large hall. All one needs to do is to place both sides' forces in their sailing formations on large, separate tables, with a further umpire's table on which is kept a map plot which shows where the two sides actually are. When an air attack is launched it is formed up over the appropriate fleet and then transferred to the umpire's plot. If and when the attacking aircraft find their target, the action is then transferred to the relevant table, and the attack is played through.

At this stage in the proceedings it is up to the game organizers to determine which of the many sets of wargames rules to use to decide the outcome of the attack. My personal preference would be to use either a suitably adapted version of F. T. Jane's *Naval "War Game" Rules* (see above) or Fletcher Pratt's *Naval War Game* (published in the U.S. in 1940). The former was used by the Japanese Navy as a training aid up until 1920, and were probably used, in an adapted form, until 1945. The latter, while never being adopted by the U.S. Navy as a training game, is contemporary with the period, was played by some U.S. Navy personnel during the Second World War, and has formed the basis for numerous rule sets since.

A more modern alternative to these two sets of rules can be found in Paul Hague's book *Naval Wargaming* (published in 1992). This book has a specific chapter which deals with the use of aircraft and aircraft carriers, and contains some interesting and novel rule concepts which deal with preparing aircraft for combat, reconnaissance, air-to-air combat, antiaircraft fire, and the effects of bomb and torpedo attacks, all of which are well worth looking at.

All the suggestions made so far deal with the more traditional style of wargaming, i.e., where models and/or maps are used. There are, however, two other methods by which part or all of the Battle of Midway can be refought. These are Board Wargames and Computer Wargames.

Board wargames have a history which goes back almost as far as the more traditional style of wargames, and in many ways they are more academic in origin. The use of hexes for movement (something which is common to almost all board wargames) was introduced just after the Second

World War by the Rand Corporation (which was set up as an operational research center for the U.S. Air Force), and the idea was copied by Charles Roberts, the founder of Avalon Hill, in the early 1950s. Since then many hundreds, if not thousands, of board wargames have been developed and played by both the military and the amateur.

Several of these games have sought to recreate all or part of the Battle of Midway. These include "Midway" [Avalon Hill (1964)], "Battle for Midway" [GDW (1976)], "Incredible Victory – The Battle for Midway, 1942" [Quarterdeck (1986)], and "Midway" [Command Magazine (1992)]. In addition, Avalon Hill has produced a simplified and revamped version of their 1964 game which has been reissued as part of the Smithsonian Series, and several of the large board wargames which deal with the Pacific War contain Battle of Midway scenarios. The range of board wargames dealing with Midway is thus as wide and as varied as any gamer could wish.

The advent of the personal computer has brought an ever widening range of computer wargames. They range from the "shoot 'em up" air combat games, some of which include the option to fight 1942 Pacific Air War dogfights, to strategic level games. The latter include "Carriers at War" and allow the solo wargamer to fight through the entire Battle of Midway in their own time. The only drawback with this type of game at present is the lack of a human opponent, but the ability to network personal computers so that players can interact with one another is on the increase, and this should mean that the future of computer wargames as a viable alternative to the traditional style of game or the board wargame is assured.

Whatever method one uses to refight the Battle of Midway, you will find the whole exercise very rewarding, especially as you will be following in the footsteps of the people who actually mounted the original operation. As was pointed out at the beginning, the Imperial Japanese Navy wargamed through the whole operation as part of the planning process. It is also well known that the chief umpire, Rear Admiral Ugaki, overturned some of the combat results obtained during the game, and this is often cited as being one of the reasons why the operation failed. In actual fact the results he overturned were concerned with the effects of high-level bombing attacks by B-17 bombers on the aircraft carriers, which in the game were very effective but in reality were not! The main problem which was thrown up by the Japanese game, and which was ignored despite the protestations of Rear Admiral Ugaki, was the possibility of a U.S. Navy aircraft carrier task force appearing on the flank of the Japanese aircraft carrier group while the bulk of the Japanese Air Striking Force was attacking Midway Island. The Planning Staff argued that this was very unlikely, and that there was an outline plan to deal with this eventuality. In reality no such plan existed, and when, as you will have seen earlier in this book, the U.S. Navy did appear on the flank, exactly as predicted in the game, the Japanese were caught unawares.

# MODERN CAMPAIGNS SERIES INDEX

*NOTE: Volume numbers are indicated by **bold** type, followed by page numbers.*